Descendants of William Kimbell

Generation 1

1. **WILLIAM[1] KIMBELL** was born about 1702 in Surrey County, Virginia. He died about 1770 in North Carolina. He married **(UNKNOWN)**. She was born in Virginia.

   William Kimbell and (unknown) had the following children:

   2.   i. BENJAMIN[2] KIMBELL was born about 1728 in Surry County, Virginia. He died on 25 Aug 1794 in Warren County, North Carolina. He married (1) MARY RANSOM, daughter of James Ransom and Grizelle Gwathmey about 1748. She was born about 1727 in Surry County, Virginia. She died before 19 Aug 1794. He married MARY SHEARIN. She died before 19 Aug 1794.

        ii. WILLIAM KIMBELL was born about 1727. He died about 21 Nov 1771 in Warren County, North Carolina. He married ELIZABETH (UNKNOWN).

        iii. DAVID KIMBELL was born about 1730.

        iv. JAMES KIMBELL was born about 1732.

        v. REBECCA KIMBELL was born about 1734. She married WILLIAM JOHNSON.

Generation 2

2. **BENJAMIN[2] KIMBELL** (William[1]) was born about 1728 in Surry County, Virginia. He died on 25 Aug 1794 in Warren County, North Carolina. He married (1) **MARY RANSOM**, daughter of James Ransom and Grizelle Gwathmey about 1748. She was born about 1727 in Surry County, Virginia. She died before 19 Aug 1794. He married **MARY SHEARIN**. She died before 19 Aug 1794.

   Notes for Benjamin Kimbell:
   Will Dated August 25, 1794, the day of Benjamin's death.

   Benjamin Kimbell and Mary Ransom had the following children:

   3.   i. BENJAMIN[3] KIMBELL was born about 1755 in North Carolina. He died on 23 Aug 1837 in Hempstead County, Arkansas. He married Mary Mosely, daughter of John Moseley and Ann Williams after 1781. She was born about 1760.

   4.   ii. DAVID KIMBELL was born about 1749 in North Carolina. He died in 1838 in Georgia. He married MARY JANE BELL. She was born in Sampson County, North Carolina.

   5.   iii. JAMES KIMBELL was born about 1751. He died in 1794 in Warren County, North Carolina. He married Frances (unknown) about 1775 in North Carolina. She was born about 1750. She died on 01 Mar 1823 in Decatur, Alabama.

   6.   iv. AMY KIMBELL was born about 1753. She married Ridley Jones, son of Francis Jones and (unknown) Ridley in 1775. He died before 1790.

   7.   v. LEONARD KIMBELL was born about 1757. He died after 1830 in Halifax County, North Carolina. He married Priscilla Harris, daughter of Charles Harris in 1780. She was born about 1747. She died before 1830.

   8.   vi. RANSOM KIMBELL was born about 1759 in North Carolina. He died in 1813 in Clarke County, Alabama. He married (1) JANE HARRIS, daughter of Isham Harris and Jane (unknown) about 1790. He married (2) ELIZABETH BALTHROP SHEARIN in 1804. She died in 1806. He married (3) (UNKNOWN) in 1807. She died in 1813.

vii.   WILLIAM KIMBELL was born about 1762. He died about 1826.

9.   viii. REBECCA KIMBELL was born about 1764 in Warren County, North Carolina. She died in 1797 in Randolph County, North Carolina. She married William Armistead, son of James Armistead and Ann (unknown) about 1790. He was born in 1762 in Elizabeth City, Virginia. He died on 01 Mar 1842 in Clark County, Alabama.

ix.   CHARLES KIMBELL was born about 1766. He died on 29 Oct 1795 in Warren County, North Carolina.

Generation 3

3.   **BENJAMIN[3] KIMBELL** (Benjamin[2], William[1]) was born about 1755 in North Carolina. He died on 23 Aug 1837 in Hempstead County, Arkansas. He married Mary Mosely, daughter of John Moseley and Ann Williams after 1781. She was born about 1760.

More About Benjamin Kimbell:
Occupation: Bet. 1795-1811; Justice of the Peace, Warren County, North Carolina Military Service: Revolutionary War

Notes for Benjamin Kimbell:
Will Dated May 8, 1837 in Halifax County, North Carolina. Will proved April 25, 1842.

Benjamin Kimbell and Mary Mosely had the following children:

10.   i. JOSEPH[4] KIMBELL was born in 1786 in Warren County, North Carolina. He died about Oct 1837 in Red River County, Republic of Texas. He married Elizabeth S. Davis, daughter of Samuel Davis and (unknown) Moody on 24 Dec 1807 in Warren County, North Carolina. She was born in 1786 in Warren County, North Carolina. She died between 09-27 Apr 1865 in Hunt County, Texas.

11.   ii. REBECCA KIMBELL was born about 1785 in North Carolina. She died before 09 Feb 1824 in Tennessee. She married Benjamin Sturdivant, son of Edward Sturdivant and (unknown) on 05 Feb 1805 in Warren County, North Carolina. He was born about 1786.

12.   iii. JOHN MOSELY KIMBELL was born about 1788 in North Carolina. He died in 1833 in Halifax County, North Carolina. He married Priscilla Avent in Jan 1823 in Nash County, North Carolina. She was born in 1793 in Nash County, North Carolina. She died in 1877 in Mississippi.

13.   iv. ANN NANCY KIMBELL was born about 1790 in Warren County, North Carolina. She died before 09 Feb 1824 in Tennessee. She married Richard Baxter, son of Nathaniel Baxter on 10 Jul 1810 in Warren County, North Carolina. He died before 1835.

14.   v. MARTHA PATSY KIMBELL was born about 1795 in Warren County, North Carolina. She died about 1835 in Halifax County, North Carolina. She married William Sturdivant on 13 Sep 1820 in Halifax County, North Carolina. He was born about 1782.

vi.   EDWARD W. KIMBELL was born about 1795 in North Carolina. He died in 1821 in Halifax County, North Carolina. He married Priscilla Avent on 17 Oct 1820. She was born in 1793 in Nash County, North Carolina. She died in 1877 in Mississippi.

vii.   WILLIAM D. KIMBELL was born about 1800. He died in 1831 in Halifax County, North Carolina. He married Emily Marshall on 21 Jan 1829 in Halifax County, North Carolina.

15.   viii. HARRISON (HENRY) JOHNSON KIMBELL was born about 1801 in Warren County, North Carolina. He died before 16 Oct 1857 in Hempstead County, Arkansas. He married Nancy A. Derring about 1831 in Nash County, North Carolina. She was born in 1810 in Nash County, North Carolina.

4.   **DAVID^3 KIMBELL** (Benjamin^2, William^1) was born about 1749 in North Carolina. He died in 1838 in Georgia. He married **MARY JANE BELL**. She was born in Sampson County, North Carolina.

David Kimbell and Mary Jane Bell had the following children:

16.   i. BENJAMIN^4 KIMBELL was born in 1778 in North Carolina. He died in 1851. He married NANCY COKELEY. He married (2) ELIZABETH CROW in 1838. She was born about 1791 in Georgia.

17.   ii. CHRISTOPHER KIMBELL was born about 1784. He married Mary Waters on 23 Oct 1819 in Oglethorpe County, Georgia.

18.   iii. GIDEON KIMBELL was born about 1786. He died about 1838. He married Anna Maxey on 18 Mar 1813 in Clark County, Georgia.

iv. THOMAS KIMBELL was born about 1792. He married NANCY THOMPSON.

v.   ROBERT KIMBELL was born about 1794. He married SARAH HINTON.

vi. RANSOM KIMBELL was born about 1798. He married MARTHA HARRIS.

vii. DAVID KIMBELL was born about 1801. He married SUSANNAH ANDERSON.

5.   **JAMES^3 KIMBELL** (Benjamin^2, William^1) was born about 1751. He died in 1794 in Warren County, North Carolina. He married Frances (unknown) about 1775 in North Carolina. She was born about 1750. She died on 01 Mar 1823 in Decatur, Alabama.

More About Frances (unknown):
Burial: Kimbell Cemetery, Decatur, Alabama

James Kimbell and Frances (unknown) had the following children:

19.   i. EDMOND^4 KIMBELL was born on 30 Jul 1777 in Warren County, North Carolina. He died on 17 Oct 1854. He married Elizabeth M. Tunstall on 01 Jan 1803. She was born on 04 Dec 1787 in Virginia. She died on 14 Nov 1849.

20.   ii. JAMES KIMBELL was born on 02 May 1781 in Warren County, North Carolina. He died on 08 Apr 1841 in Decatur, Alabama. He married Nancy Burt, daughter of William Burt about 1810 in Halifax, North carolina. She was born in 1785 in Halifax County, North Carolina. She died on 04 Jan 1855 in Decatur, Alabama.

21.   iii. NATHAN KIMBELL was born about 1783. He died before 1850 in Morgan County, Alabama. He married Sarah Peyton on 26 Feb 1812 in Cumberland County, North carolina. She was born in 1793 in North Carolina.

22.   iv. MARY KIMBELL was born on 11 Aug 1788. She died on 13 Oct 1824. She married

George Murphy on 13 Oct 1806. He was born in 1774. He died in 1846.

6. **AMY**[3] **KIMBELL** (Benjamin[2], William[1]) was born about 1753. She married Ridley Jones, son of Francis Jones and (unknown) Ridley in 1775. He died before 1790.

    Ridley Jones and Amy Kimbell had the following child:
    i.   MARY[4] JONES.

7. **LEONARD**[3] **KIMBELL** (Benjamin[2], William[1]) was born about 1757. He died after 1830 in Halifax County, North Carolina. He married Priscilla Harris, daughter of Charles Harris in 1780. She was born about 1747. She died before 1830.

    Leonard Kimbell and Priscilla Harris had the following child:
    i.   WILLIAM[4] KIMBELL.

8. **RANSOM**[3] **KIMBELL** (Benjamin[2], William[1]) was born about 1759 in North Carolina. He died in 1813 in Clarke County, Alabama. He married (1) **JANE HARRIS**, daughter of Isham Harris and Jane (unknown) about 1790. He married (2) **ELIZABETH BALTHROP SHEARIN** in 1804. She died in 1806. He married (3) **(UNKNOWN)** in 1807. She died in 1813.

    Ransom Kimbell and Jane Harris had the following children:
    i.   JOHN H.[4] KIMBELL was born on 18 Mar 1791.

    24. ii. ISHAM KIMBELL was born on 31 Mar 1797 in Warren County, North Carolina. He died on 17 Feb 1881 in Jackson, Alabama. He married Martha T. Carney, daughter of Josiah Carney and Sarah (unknown) in 1821. She was born on 26 Dec 1797 in North Carolina. She died on 02 Jun 1853 in Jackson, Alabama.

    iii. TABITHA KIMBELL was born on 01 Sep 1799.

    iv.   JAMES H. KIMBELL was born on 23 Sep 1801.

9. **REBECCA**[3] **KIMBELL** (Benjamin[2], William[1]) was born about 1764 in Warren County, North Carolina. She died in 1797 in Randolph County, North Carolina. She married William Armistead, son of James Armistead and Ann (unknown) about 1790. He was born in 1762 in Elizabeth City, Virginia. He died on 01 Mar 1842 in Clark County, Alabama.

    More About William Armistead:
    Military Service: Revolutionary War

    William Armistead and Rebecca Kimbell had the following children:
    i.   WESTWOOD[4] ARMISTEAD was born on 24 Aug 1791 in Randolph County, North Carolina. He died in Feb 1845 in Alabama. He married ELIZABETH BOROUGHS. She was born about 1793. She died on 06 May 1879.

    ii. JOHN KIMBELL ARMISTEAD was born on 16 Dec 1792. He married JULIE GAINES.

    25. iii. ELIZABETH LEE ARMISTEAD was born on 13 Oct 1794 in Warren County, North Carolina. She died in 1841 in Clarke County, Alabama. She married JOHN MORRISS. He died in 1819.

    iv.   MARTHA JANE ARMISTEAD was born on 01 Sep 1796. She married EDMUND WADDILL.

10.   JOSEPH[4] KIMBELL (Benjamin[3], Benjamin[2], William[1]) was born in 1786 in Warren County, North Carolina. He died about Oct 1837 in Red River County, Republic of Texas. He married Elizabeth S. Davis, daughter of Samuel Davis and (unknown) Moody on 24 Dec 1807 in Warren County, North Carolina. She was born in 1786 in Warren County, North Carolina. She died between 09-27 Apr 1865 in Hunt County, Texas.

More About Joseph Kimbell:
Burial: Compton Cemetery, (near) Roxton, Texas
Occupation: Farmer
Occupation: Surveyor

Notes for Joseph Kimbell:
Arrived in Republic of Texas September 25, 1837.

More About Joseph Kimbell and Elizabeth S. Davis:
Marriage Fact: 24 Dec 1807 in Warren County, North Carolina; Date of Marriage Bond. Ransom Kimbell Bondsman

Joseph Kimbell and Elizabeth S. Davis had the following children:

25.   i.   BENJAMIN DAVIS[5] KIMBELL was born on 28 Feb 1809 in Warren County, North Carolina. He died in Jan 1894 in Whiteflat, Texas. He married (1) S.M. HARMON on 16 Nov 1841 in Lamar County, Republic of Texas. She died before 02 Dec 1847. He married (2) AMELIA W. MOORE on 02 Dec 1847 in Cass County, Texas. She was born on 10 Mar 1829 in Alabama. She died on 24 Sep 1889 in Grange Hall, Texas.

26.   ii. THOMAS MOODY KIMBELL was born on 17 Aug 1810 in Warren County, North Carolina. He died on 23 Jan 1884 in Campbell, Texas. He married (1) ANN ELIZABETH PATILLO, daughter of Zachariah Patillo and Mary Jordan on 19 Nov 1837 in Caswell County, North Carolina. She was born in 1810. She died about 1848 in Cass County, Texas. He married (2) ANN ELIZABETH WICKER, daughter of John Wicker and Harriet (unknown) on 23 Dec 1851 in Avinger, Texas. She was born on 19 Apr 1829 in Alabama. She died on 31 Dec 1899 in Campbell, Texas.

27.   iii. JOHN M. KIMBELL was born about 1812 in Milledgeville, Tennessee. He died in Oct 1886 in Texas. He married (1) SARAH ANGELINA ELLIOTT, daughter of Richard McDowell Johnson Elliott and Jane McCullough on 05 Oct 1842 in Bowie County, Texas. She was born on 30 Oct 1825 in Holly Springs, Mississippi. She died in Apr 1864 in Bowie County, Texas. He married (2) EMMA FRANCES KNIGHT, daughter of Matthew Jouette Knight and Cecilia Amelia Ellis after Apr 1864. She was born on 23 Oct 1824 in Virginia. She died on 02 May 1879 in Bowie County, Texas.

28.   iv. REBECCA TENNESSEE KIMBELL was born in 1814 in Tennessee. She died in 1886 in Campbell, Hunt County, Texas. She married Wiley Blunt Brigham, son of David Brigham about 1838. He was born in 1805 in Tennessee. He died in 1861 in Campbell, Hunt County, Texas.

29.   v.   ALBERT GALLATIN KIMBELL was born on 20 Jan 1817 in (near) Nashville, Tennessee. He died on 20 Jun 1899 in Perris, California. He married Sarah Castain Gleaves on 12 Oct 1841 in Red River County, Republic of Texas. She was born on 15 May 1825 in Davidson county, Tennessee. She died on 02 Dec 1880 in California.

      vi. NANCY ANNE KIMBELL was born in 1818 in Tennessee. She died on 04 Sep 1838 in Red River County, Republic of Texas.

Notes for Nancy Anne Kimbell:
Did Not Marry.

30.   vii. WILLIAM H. KIMBELL was born in 1822 in Tennessee. He died on 01 May 1853 in Austin, Texas. He married Rebecca A. (unknown) about 1848. She was born on 17 Sep 1833 in Tennessee. She died on 19 Dec 1908 in Texas.

         viii. HENRY STOKES KIMBELL was born in 1824 in Dixon County, Tennessee. He died after 14 Jun 1880 in Pomona, California.

More About Henry Stokes Kimbell:
Living In: 1880 Living in the home of W. G. Bartlett in San Jose, Los Angeles County, California.
Occupation: 14 Nov 1850 in Marin County, California; Farmer
Occupation: 1866 in Walker Basin, Kern County, California; Miner
Occupation: 1879 in Los Angeles County, California; Bee Rancher
Occupation: 1880 in San Jose, Los Angeles County, California; Apiarian (Bee Keeper)

Notes for Henry Stokes Kimbell:
Went to California during the Gold Rush of 1849. Probably arrived by ship with his brother, Albert, in January 1850.

         ix. EDWARD KIMBELL was born in 1825. He died about 1841.

11.   **REBECCA**[4] **KIMBELL** (Benjamin[3], Benjamin[2], William[1]) was born about 1785 in North Carolina. She died before 09 Feb 1824 in Tennessee. She married Benjamin Sturdivant, son of Edward Sturdivant and (unknown) on 05 Feb 1805 in Warren County, North Carolina. He was born about 1786.

Benjamin Sturdivant and Rebecca Kimbell had the following children:

         i. (DAUGHTER)[5] STURDIVANT was born in 1806 in Warren County, North Carolina.

32.   ii. JOSEPH E. STURDIVANT was born in 1808 in Warren County, North Carolina. He died in 1876 in Marion County, Texas. He married NANCY ANN COOPWOOD. She was born about 1815.

         iii. ELIZABETH STURDIVANT was born in 1810 in Warren County, North Carolina. She died in Marshall County, Mississippi. She married WILLIAM T. COOPWOOD.

         iv. MICHAEL C. M. STURDIVANT was born in 1812. He died in 1839 in Marshall County, Mississippi.

12.   **JOHN MOSELY**[4] **KIMBELL** (Benjamin[3], Benjamin[2], William[1]) was born about 1788 in North Carolina. He died in 1833 in Halifax County, North Carolina. He married Priscilla Avent in Jan 1823 in Nash County, North Carolina. She was born in 1793 in Nash County, North Carolina. She died in 1877 in Mississippi.

More About Priscilla Avent:
b: 1793

John Mosely Kimbell and Priscilla Avent had the following children:

32.   i. MARTHA FRANCES[5] KIMBELL was born about 1826 in Halifax County, North Carolina. She died in 1896 in Mississippi. She married REDDING HERVEY.

       ii.   JOSEPH W. KIMBELL was born about 1828 in Halifax County, North Carolina. He died after 1883 in Halifax County, North Carolina.

33.   iii. SALLY ANN KIMBELL was born about 1832 in Halifax County, North Carolina. She died in 1852 in Mississippi. She married Lafayette L. Moore about 1848 in Halifax County, North Carolina.

13. **ANN NANCY[4] KIMBELL** (Benjamin[3], Benjamin[2], William[1]) was born about 1790 in Warren County, North Carolina. She died before 09 Feb 1824 in Tennessee. She married Richard Baxter, son of Nathaniel Baxter on 10 Jul 1810 in Warren County, North Carolina. He died before 1835.

Richard Baxter and Ann Nancy Kimbell had the following children:

       i.   PERMELIA[5] BAXTER. She married (UNKNOWN) MOORE.

       ii.   MARY BAXTER. She married (UNKNOWN) SARCY.

       iii.   MARTHA BAXTER. She married (UNKNOWN) YOUNG.

       iv.   NATHANIEL BAXTER.

       v.   EDWARD BAXTER. He died in 1838 in Cass County, Texas.

14. **MARTHA PATSY[4] KIMBELL** (Benjamin[3], Benjamin[2], William[1]) was born about 1795 in Warren County, North Carolina. She died about 1835 in Halifax County, North Carolina. She married William Sturdivant on 13 Sep 1820 in Halifax County, North Carolina. He was born about 1782.

William Sturdivant and Martha Patsy Kimbell had the following children:

       i.   CATHERINE[5] STURDIVANT. She married WILLIAM T. WILLIAMS.

       ii.   REBECCA STURDIVANT.

       iii.   PERMELIA STURDIVANT.

       iv.   ROBERT STURDIVANT. He died in 1845.

       v.   BENJAMIN STURDIVANT.

       vi.   SALLY STURDIVANT.

15. **HARRISON (HENRY) JOHNSON[4] KIMBELL** (Benjamin[3], Benjamin[2], William[1]) was born about 1801 in Warren County, North Carolina. He died before 16 Oct 1857 in Hempstead County, Arkansas. He married Nancy A. Derring about 1831 in Nash County, North Carolina. She was born in 1810 in Nash County, North Carolina.

More About Harrison (Henry) Johnson Kimbell:
Occupation: 1850 in Ozan, Hempstead County, Arkansas; Farmer

Harrison (Henry) Johnson Kimbell and Nancy A. Derring had the following children:
       i.   MARY J.[5] KIMBELL was born about 1832 in North Carolina.

ii. JOHN D. KIMBELL was born on 02 Nov 1834 in North Carolina. He died on 16 Oct 1901 in Arkansas. He married MARY JOSEPHINE LANGTREE. She was born on 08 Dec 1840 in Arkansas. She died on 08 May 1870 in Little Rock, Pulaski County, Arkansas.

More About John D. Kimbell:
Burial: Mount Holly Cemetery, Little Rock, Pulaski County, Arkansas

iii. SARAH E. KIMBELL was born about 1836 in North Carolina.

iv. MARTHA A. KIMBELL was born about 1838 in North Carolina.

v. JOSEPH W. KIMBELL was born about 1840 in Arkansas.

vi. WILLIAM H. KIMBELL was born about 1842 in Arkansas.

16. BENJAMIN[4] KIMBELL (David[3], Benjamin[2], William[1]) was born in 1778 in North Carolina. He died in 1851. He married NANCY COKELEY. He married (2) ELIZABETH CROW in 1838. She was born about 1791 in Georgia.

Benjamin Kimbell and Nancy Cokeley had the following children:

34. i. WILLIAM[5] KIMBELL was born in 1805 in North Carolina. He married MARY HENTON.

ii. JOHN KIMBELL.

iii. FRANCES KIMBELL. She married ISAAC HAND. He was born in 1806.

iv. MARY KIMBELL. She married JAMES MOORE.

v. NANCY KIMBELL. She married A. C. FARRELL.

17. CHRISTOPHER[4] KIMBELL (David[3], Benjamin[2], William[1]) was born about 1784. He married Mary Waters on 23 Oct 1819 in Oglethorpe County, Georgia.

Christopher Kimbell and Mary Waters had the following children:

i. WILLIAM LUMPKIN[5] KIMBELL was born on 17 Sep 1820. He married (1) MINERVA ROBERTSON in 1846. She was born in 1819. She died in 1875. He married SAMANTHA THROVER. She was born in 1837. She died in 1888.

ii. MARTHA KIMBELL. She married THESBY CRONE.

iii. DAVID T. KIMBELL.

iv. MARY M. KIMBELL. She married ROBERT CHAPPELL.

v. GEORGE W. KIMBELL.

vi. AMELIA FRANCES KIMBELL. She married ARCHIBALD BROWN.

vii. CHRISTOPHER J. KIMBELL.

viii. ELIZABETH KIMBELL was born on 08 Jan 1835. She married THOMAS M. SULLIVAN.

    ix.   SARAH B. KIMBELL was born on 01 Aug 1839. She died on 24 Apr 1913. She married J. C. McDaniel on 12 Aug 1866.

    x.   JOHN B. KIMBELL was born in 1840. He died in 1915.

18.   **GIDEON[4] KIMBELL** (David[3], Benjamin[2], William[1]) was born about 1786. He died about 1838. He married Anna Maxey on 18 Mar 1813 in Clark County, Georgia.

Gideon Kimbell and Anna Maxey had the following children:

    i.   FINNEY[5] KIMBELL.

36.   ii. JOHN THOMAS KIMBELL was born on 12 Jan 1814 in Oglethorpe County, Georgia. He died on 05 Jul 1899. He married Mary Pittman Lumpkin on 27 Mar 1834 in Georgia. She was born on 16 Mar 1810. She died on 26 Jan 1888 in Georgia.

    iii.   ELIZA K. KIMBELL was born about 1815.

    iv.   MARY G. KIMBELL was born about 1815.

    v.   JOSEPH WALKER KIMBELL was born about 1817. He married ELIZABETH BRYANT. He married MARTHA LUMPKIN.

    vi.   ANN KIMBELL was born about 1818.

    vii.   NATHANIEL KIMBELL was born about 1820.

    viii.   SARAH B. KIMBELL was born on 01 Apr 1821. She died on 05 Oct 1875. She married DAVID ASBURY.

    ix.   JAMES GRAHAM KIMBELL was born on 30 May 1823. He married Martha Anderson on 17 Nov 1842 in Georgia.

    More About James Graham Kimbell:
    Occupation: ; Baptist Minister

    x.   FRANCES M. KIMBELL was born in 1825.

    xi.   LUCY L. KIMBELL was born about 1835.

    xii.   MARTHA F. KIMBELL was born about 1835. She died on 16 Aug 1888. She married (UNKNOWN) MCKIBBEN.

19.   **EDMOND[4] KIMBELL** (James[3], Benjamin[2], William[1]) was born on 30 Jul 1777 in Warren County, North Carolina. He died on 17 Oct 1854. He married Elizabeth M. Tunstall on 01 Jan 1803. She was born on 04 Dec 1787 in Virginia. She died on 14 Nov 1849.

More About Edmond Kimbell:
Burial: Kimbell Cemetery, Decatur, Alabama

More About Elizabeth M. Tunstall:

Burial: Kimbell Cemetery, Decatur, Alabama

Edmond Kimbell and Elizabeth M. Tunstall had the following children:

36.   i.   MARY C.[5] KIMBELL was born about 1805. She married Peyton H. Lyles in 1824.

       ii.   PERLEMINA KIMBELL was born between 1813-1817 in Alabama. She died in 1856.

37.   iii. FRANCES A. KIMBELL was born on 31 Jan 1817. She died on 15 Aug 1859. She married JOHN PATRICK MOSELEY.

       iv.   WILLIAM KIMBELL was born in 1821 in Alabama. He died in 1853.

       v.   MARTHA KIMBELL was born in 1825 in Alabama.

More About Martha Kimbell:
Burial: Kimbell Cemetery, Decatur, Alabama

20.   **JAMES[4] KIMBELL** (James[3], Benjamin[2], William[1]) was born on 02 May 1781 in Warren County, North Carolina. He died on 08 Apr 1841 in Decatur, Alabama. He married Nancy Burt, daughter of William Burt about 1810 in Halifax, North carolina. She was born in 1785 in Halifax County, North Carolina. She died on 04 Jan 1855 in Decatur, Alabama.

More About James Kimbell:
Burial: Kimbell Cemetery, Decatur, Alabama

More About Nancy Burt:
Burial: Kimbell Cemetery, Decatur, Alabama

James Kimbell and Nancy Burt had the following children:

       i.   MARY BURT[5] KIMBELL was born on 01 Sep 1817. She died on 10 Sep 1826 in Decatur, Alabama.

More About Mary Burt Kimbell:
Burial: Kimbell Cemetery, Decatur, Alabama

       ii.   JAMES H. KIMBELL was born on 22 Nov 1819. He died on 22 Aug 1825 in Decatur, Alabama.

More About James H. Kimbell:
Burial: Kimbell Cemetery, Decatur, Alabama

       iii. EDWIN KIMBELL was born on 26 Sep 1826. He died on 14 Nov 1887.

More About Edwin Kimbell:
Burial: Kimbell Cemetery, Decatur, Alabama

       iv. ELIZA REBECCA KIMBELL was born between 1826-1829. She died in Decatur, Alabama. She married William Wilson on 29 Aug 1855.

More About Eliza Rebecca Kimbell:
Burial: Kimbell Cemetery, Decatur, Alabama

     v.   SARAH KIMBELL was born in 1829. She died in 1890. She married T. J. McDaniel in 1863.

21.   **NATHAN**[4] **KIMBELL** (James[3], Benjamin[2], William[1]) was born about 1783. He died before 1850 in Morgan County, Alabama. He married Sarah Peyton on 26 Feb 1812 in Cumberland County, North carolina. She was born in 1793 in North Carolina.

More About Nathan Kimbell:
Occupation: Minister

Nathan Kimbell and Sarah Peyton had the following children:

38.   i.   MARY P.[5] KIMBELL was born in 1814. She married EDWARD LOGWOOD. She married ATABALPA COLUMBUS STUART.

     ii.   THOMAS P. KIMBELL was born in 1818.

     iii.   SARAH FRANCES KIMBELL was born in 1824. She died in 1859. She married (UNKNOWN) SEWELL.

     iv.   JAMES W. KIMBELL was born in 1825.

     v.   FRANCIS ASBURY KIMBELL was born on 25 Aug 1829 in Morgan County, Alabama. He died on 12 Feb 1878 in Atlanta, Georgia. He married FRANCES (UNKNOWN).

          More About Francis Asbury Kimbell:
          Occupation: Minister

22.   **MARY**[4] **KIMBELL** (James[3], Benjamin[2], William[1]) was born on 11 Aug 1788. She died on 13 Oct 1824. She married George Murphy on 13 Oct 1806. He was born in 1774. He died in 1846.

More About Mary Kimbell:
Burial: Kimbell Cemetery, Decatur, Alabama

More About George Murphy:
Burial: Kimbell Cemetery, Decatur, Alabama

George Murphy and Mary Kimbell had the following children:

     i.   ELIZA M.[5] MURPHY was born on 04 Apr 1808. She died on 10 Aug 1832.

          More About Eliza M. Murphy:
          Burial: Kimbell Cemetery, Decatur, Alabama

     ii.   NATHAN KIMBELL MURPHY was born on 29 Mar 1810. He died on 11 Nov 1858 in Decatur, Alabama.

          More About Nathan Kimbell Murphy:
          Burial: Kimbell Cemetery, Decatur, Alabama

iii.   TEMPERANCE HILL MURPHY was born on 04 May 1814. She died on 01 Oct 1836.

More About Temperance Hill Murphy: Burial:
Kimbell Cemetery, Decatur, Alabama

iv.   MARY FRANCES MURPHY was born on 24 Jan 1817. She died on 17 Oct 1838.

More About Mary Frances Murphy:
Burial: Kimbell Cemetery, Decatur, Alabama

23.   ISHAM[4] KIMBELL (Ransom[3], Benjamin[2], William[1]) was born on 31 Mar 1797 in Warren County, North Carolina. He died on 17 Feb 1881 in Jackson, Alabama. He married Martha T. Carney, daughter of Josiah Carney and Sarah (unknown) in 1821. She was born on 26 Dec 1797 in North Carolina. She died on 02 Jun 1853 in Jackson, Alabama.

More About Isham Kimbell:
Burial: Pine Crest Cemetery, Jackson, Alabama
Occupation: 1819; Operated a Mercantile Business in Jackson, Alabama
Occupation: Bet. 1833-1850; Clerk of the Circuit Court, Clarke County, Alabama
Occupation: Postmaster, Jackson, Alabama
Occupation: Sheriff, Clarke County, Alabama

More About Martha T. Carney:
Burial: Pine Crest Cemetery, Jackson, Alabama

Isham Kimbell and Martha T. Carney had the following children:

i.   THOMAS ISHAM[5] KIMBELL was born on 10 May 1829 in Clarke County, Alabama. He died on 11 Feb 1914 in Clarke County, Alabama. He married MARTHA JANE BOROUGHS. She was born on 15 Jan 1838 in Clarke County, Alabama. She died on 17 Jun 1903 in Clarke County, Alabama.

More About Thomas Isham Kimbell:
Military Service: Company E, 24th Alabama Infantry, C. S. A.

Notes for Thomas Isham Kimbell:
Served as Lieutenant and then Captain of Company E, 24th Alabama Infantry. Commisioned Captain on September 19, 1862.
Paroled on May 24, 1865 after 24th Alabama Infantry was surrendered.by General Taylor, C.S.A..

ii.   SARAH ANN KIMBELL was born in 1822. She died in 1899. She married ARCHIE SMOOT.

iii.   MARTHA ELVIRA KIMBELL was born in 1823. She died in 1874. She married E. M. PORTIS.

iv.   JOHN CARNEY KIMBELL was born in 1825. He died in 1904. He married MARTHA ARMISTEAD WILLIAMS.

v.   MARY E. KIMBELL was born in 1827. She died in 1893.

Notes for Mary E. Kimbell:
Never Married.

vi.   CAROLINE AMELIA KIMBELL was born in 1834. She died in 1920.

Notes for Caroline Amelia
Kimbell: Never Married.

vii.   REBECCA CARNEY KIMBELL was born in 1837. She died in 1864. She married JOHN CALHOUN CHAPMAN.

24.   ELIZABETH LEE[4] ARMISTEAD (Rebecca[3] Kimbell, Benjamin[2] Kimbell, William[1] Kimbell) was born on 13 Oct 1794 in Warren County, North Carolina. She died in 1841 in Clarke County, Alabama. She married JOHN MORRISS. He died in 1819.

Notes for John Morriss:
Never returned from a trip to Alabama in 1819 and presumed killed.

John Morriss and Elizabeth Lee Armistead had the following children:

39.   i. REBECCA M.[5] MORRISS was born in Randolph County, North Carolina. She died on 08 Sep 1862 in Clarke County, Alabama. She married THOMAS BOROUGHS. He was born on 11 Aug 1803 in North Carolina. He died on 02 Nov 1866 in Clarke County, Alabama.

ii.   GEORGE WASHINGTON MORRISS.

iii.   WILLIAM MORRISS.

iv.   MARTHA JANE MORRISS. She married SAMUEL FORWOOD.

Generation 5

25.   BENJAMIN DAVIS[5] KIMBELL (Joseph[4], Benjamin[3], Benjamin[2], William[1]) was born on 28 Feb 1809 in Warren County, North Carolina. He died in Jan 1894 in Whiteflat, Texas. He married (1) S.M. HARMON on 16 Nov 1841 in Lamar County, Republic of Texas. She died before 02 Dec 1847. He married (2) AMELIA W. MOORE on 02 Dec 1847 in Cass County, Texas. She was born on 10 Mar 1829 in Alabama. She died on 24 Sep 1889 in Grange Hall, Texas.

More About Benjamin Davis Kimbell:
Burial: White Flat Cemetery, Whiteflat, Motley County, Texas
Occupation: 04 Oct 1838; Sworn in as acting Justice of the Peace in Lamar County, Texas
Occupation: 1860 in Hill County, Texas; Blacksmith
Occupation: 1870 in Precinct 3, Hill County, Texas;
Farmer
Occupation: 1880 in Hill County, Texas; Farmer
Occupation: Surveyor for Cass County, Texas
Property: 24 May 1848 in Lamar County, Texas; 320 Acres
Property: 1850 in Cass County, Texas; 25 Acres Improved and 295 Acres Unimproved
Property: 1860 in Hill County, Texas; 1 Acre Improved and 20 Acres Unimproved
Property: 1880 in Hill County, Texas; 83 Acres Improved and 164 Acres Unimproved

Notes for Benjamin Davis Kimbell:

Arrived in Republic of Texas October 30, 1837.

Benjamin Davis Kimbell and S.M. Harmon had the following child:

    i.   TENNESSEE LOU[6] KIMBELL was born in 1842 in Texas. She died in Paducah, Texas. She married (UNKNOWN) POWELL.

More About Amelia W. Moore:
Burial: Dodson Cemetery, Hill County, Texas

Benjamin Davis Kimbell and Amelia W. Moore had the following children:

40.   ii. EDWARD BASCOM KIMBELL was born on 26 Aug 1848 in Cass County, Texas. He died on 06 Jan 1925 in Whiteflat, Texas. He married Missouri Alice Turner, daughter of John Gilead Rupe Turner and Hester Ann Megee on 12 May 1874 in Milford, Texas. She was born on 13 Nov 1853 in Ellis County, Texas. She died on 17 Apr 1935.

41.   iii. GEORGE WASHINGTON KIMBELL was born on 17 Aug 1850 in Cass County, Texas. He died on 10 Jul 1921 in Flomot, Texas. He married (1) CLEMMIE MAXWELL on 12 May 1874 in Milford, Texas. She died in 1884. He married (2) DIXIE RANSONE in 1886. She was born on 09 Nov 1862 in Cleburne, Texas. She died on 23 Sep 1903 in Motley County, Texas.

42.   iv. MATILDA KIMBELL was born on 29 May 1852. She died on 08 Sep 1888 in Lampasas, Texas. She married BAILEY BAKER.

    v. JOSEPHENE M. KIMBELL was born on 13 Oct 1854 in Hill County, Texas. She died on 26 Dec 1872 in Dodson Cemetery, Hill County, Texas.

    vi. JEFFERSON D. KIMBELL was born on 07 May 1859 in Hill County, Texas. He died on 26 Oct 1866 in Dodson , Hill County, Texas.

More About Jefferson D. Kimbell:
Burial: Dodson Cemetery, Hill County, Texas

43.   vii. WILLIAM BAYLESS KIMBELL was born on 23 May 1865 in Blum, Texas. He died on 12 Jun 1928 in Dimmitt, Texas. He married Margaret Elizabeth Vashti Bankston, daughter of Jackson Washington Bankston and Nancy Elizabeth Thurman on 29 Jan 1891 in Floydada, Texas. She was born on 05 Feb 1869 in Walker County, Georgia. She died on 18 Jul 1936 in Dimmiitt, Texas.

26. THOMAS MOODY[5] KIMBELL (Joseph[4], Benjamin[3], Benjamin[2], William[1]) was born on 17 Aug 1810 in Warren County, North Carolina. He died on 23 Jan 1884 in Campbell, Texas. He married (1) ANN ELIZABETH PATILLO, daughter of Zachariah Patillo and Mary Jordan on 19 Nov 1837 in Caswell County, North Carolina. She was born in 1810. She died about 1848 in Cass County, Texas. He married (2) ANN ELIZABETH WICKER, daughter of John Wicker and Harriet (unknown) on 23 Dec 1851 in Avinger, Texas. She was born on 19 Apr 1829 in Alabama. She died on 31 Dec 1899 in Campbell, Texas.

More About Thomas Moody Kimbell:

Burial: Brigham Cemetery, Hunt County, Texas
Occupation: 14 Feb 1848; Appointed Postmaster of Hickory Hill, Texas
Occupation: 1850 in Precinct 2, Cass County, Texas; Farmer

Occupation: 1860 in Precinct 2, Hunt County, Texas; Farmer
Occupation: 1880 in Precinct 4, Hunt County, Texas;
Farmer
Occupation: Surveyor
Property: 1860 in Hunt County, Texas; 30 Acres Improved and 612 Acres Unimproved
Property: 1870 in Hunt County, Texas; 60 Acres Improved and 26 Acres Unimproved
Property: 1880 in Hunt County, Texas; 132 Acres Improved and 100 Acres Unimproved

Notes for Thomas Moody Kimbell:
Arrived in Republic ofTexas January 20,
1837.
Willl Dated November 24, 1883.
Took the Oath of Allegiance to the Repubic of Texas on October 4, 1838. Oath was given by H.
L. Williams, Justice of the Peace, Red River County, Republic of Texas.

Thomas Moody Kimbell and Ann Elizabeth Patillo had the following children:

     i.   JOSEPH[6] KIMBELL was born about 1842 in Cass County, Republic of Texas. He died in 1856 in Cass County, Texas.

           More About Joseph Kimbell:
           Cause Of Death: Typhoid

44.   ii. HELENA TEXANA KIMBELL was born on 16 Feb 1845 in Hickory Hill, Cass County, Republic of Texas. She died in 1908. She married Robert Sayle on 28 Sep 1866. He was born on 14 Jan 1831. He died in Jul 1914 in Greenville, Texas.

45.   iii. MARY ANN ELIZABETH KIMBELL was born on 23 Dec 1848 in Cass County, Texas. She died on 05 Jul 1881 in Hunt County, Texas. She married Benjamin Franklin Kelly on 02 Mar 1869 in Hunt County, Texas. He was born on 17 Dec 1844 in Charleston, Virginia. He died on 10 Mar 1896 in Commerce, Texas.

More About Ann Elizabeth Wicker:
Burial: Brigham Cemetery, Hunt County, Texas

More About Thomas Moody Kimbell and Ann Elizabeth Wicker:
Marriage Fact: Married in the home of the bride by J. A. Zinn.

Thomas Moody Kimbell and Ann Elizabeth Wicker had the following children:

46.   iv. CHARLES HENRY KIMBELL was born on 16 Jan 1855 in Cass County, Texas. He died on 20 Oct 1926 in Campbell, Texas. He married Laura Lou Taylor on 16 Aug 1909 in Greenville, Texas. She was born on 25 Aug 1884 in Dukedom, Kentucky. She died on 26 Oct 1982 in Greenville, Texas.

47.   v. MARTHA REBECCA KIMBELL was born on 30 Sep 1856 in Cass County, Texas. She died on 18 Jul 1888. She married Robert Wright Ridley on 12 Feb 1880. He was born in 1839. He died in 1918.

     vi.   HATTIE LEE KIMBELL was born on 07 Feb 1864 in Hunt County, Texas. She died on 20 Jul 1920 in Bellaire, Harris County, Texas. She married THOMAS JOSEPH PATILLO. He died on 27 Mar 1926 in Houston, Texas.

           More About Hattie Lee Kimbell:
           Burial: Brigham Cemetery, Campbell, Texas

27. **John M.**[5] **Kimbell** (Joseph[4], Benjamin[3], Benjamin[2], William[1]) was born about 1812 in Milledgeville, Tennessee. He died in Oct 1886 in Texas. He married (1) **Sarah Angelina Elliott**, daughter of Richard McDowell Johnson Elliott and Jane McCullough on 05 Oct 1842 in Bowie County, Texas. She was born on 30 Oct 1825 in Holly Springs, Mississippi. She died in Apr 1864 in Bowie County, Texas. He married (2) **Emma Frances Knight**, daughter of Matthew Jouette Knight and Cecilia Amelia Ellis after Apr 1864. She was born on 23 Oct 1824 in Virginia. She died on 02 May 1879 in Bowie County, Texas.

More About John M. Kimbell:
Living In: 1846 Bowie County, Texas
Living In: Bet. 1850-1880 Bowie County, Texas
Occupation: Bet. 07 Jan-26 May 1847 in Dekalb, Texas; Postmaster
Occupation: Bet. 19 Jul 1848-19 Aug 1864 in Dekalb, Texas; Postmaster
Occupation: 1850 in District 8, Bowie County, Texas; Blacksmith
Occupation: 1860 in DeKalb, Bowie County, Texas; Blacksmith and Hotel Owner
Occupation: 1870 in Precinct 4, Bowie County, Texas; Farmer
Occupation: 1880 in Bowie County, Texas; Mechanic
Property: 1851 in Bowie County, Texas; 210 Acres and two town lots in DeKalb.
Property: 1858 in Bowie County, Texas; 675 Acres. Three town lots in DeKalb and two town lots in Boston.
Property: 1860 in Bowie County, Texas; 730 Acres and one town lot in DeKalb.
Property: 1864 in Bowie County, Texas; 730 Acres
Property: 1865 in Bowie County, Texas; 730 Acres and one town lot in DeKalb.
Property: 1866 in Bowie County, Texas; 730 Acres and one town lot in DeKalb.
Property: 1866 in Lamar County, Texas; 270 Acres (Soldier's Claim)
Property: 1867 in Bowie County, Texas; 730 Acres and one town lot in DeKalb. Property: 1868 in Bowie County, Texas; 460 Acres
Property: 1869 in Bowie County, Texas; 460 Acres
Property: 1870 in Bowie County, Texas; 100 Acres Improved and 340 Acres Unimproved
Property: 1873 in Cass County, Texas; 150 Acres (from R.M.J. Elliott)
Property: 1875 in Cass County, Texas; 43.5 Acres (from R.M.J. Elliott)
Property: 1875 in Lamar County, Texas; 65 Acres
Property: 1875 in Bowie County, Texas; 262.5 Acres
Property: 1878 in Bowie County, Texas; 120 Acres
Property: 1879 in Bowie County, Texas; 120 Acres
  Notes for John M. Kimbell:
Moved to Dekalb, Texas in 1832.
Gave Oath of Allegiance to the Republic of Texas in May 1837.

Notes for Sarah Angelina Elliott:
Died while giving birth to John D. Kimbell.

John M. Kimbell and Sarah Angelina Elliott had the following children:

48.   i. **Elizabeth Jane**[6] **Kimbell** was born on 23 Jul 1843 in DeKalb, Republic of Texas. She died on 08 Feb 1920 in Texarkana, Bowie County, Texas. She married Rhesa Walker Read, son of Martin I. Read and Eliza Walker on 16 Nov 1859 in DeKalb, Texas. He was born on 20 Dec 1836 in Canton, Alabama. He died on 02 Aug 1909 in Texarkana, Bowie County, Texas.

49.   ii. **Julia Rebecca Kimbell** was born on 31 Mar 1845 in Republic of Texas. She died on 26 Jan 1908 in Texas. She married (1) **Edward Warren Garland**, son of Edward Garland and Nancy W. Smiser before 1878. He was born on 28 Oct 1825 in Giles County, Tennessee. He died on 12 May 1897 in Texas. She married (2)

WILLIAM J. WYSE, son of James William Wyse and Patience Caroline Baker Teel after 07 May 1865. He was born in 1830 in Louisiana.

50.   iii. MARY EMMA KIMBELL was born on 26 Mar 1847 in Texas. She died on 14 Apr 1922 in Deport, Lamar County, Texas. She married Robert J. Bevill before 15 Jul 1870. He was born on 13 Mar 1847 in Henderson, Tennessee. He died on 09 Jan 1913 in Lamar County, Texas.

51.   iv. EMILY MATILDA KIMBELL was born in 1850 in DeKalb, Bowie County, Texas. She died on 13 Apr 1928 in Texarkana, Bowie County, Texas. She married James Joseph Peters, son of Lemuel Peters and Elizabeth (unknown) on 16 Apr 1874 in Bowie County, Texas. He was born on 17 Dec 1843 in Bowie County, Texas. He died on 10 Apr 1925 in New Boston, Texas.

     v. JOHN D. KIMBELL was born in 1864 in Texas. He died after 03 Jun 1880.

28.   **REBECCA TENNESSEE[5] KIMBELL** (Joseph[4], Benjamin[3], Benjamin[2], William[1]) was born in 1814 in Tennessee. She died in 1886 in Campbell, Hunt County, Texas. She married Wiley Blunt Brigham, son of David Brigham about 1838. He was born in 1805 in Tennessee. He died in 1861 in Campbell, Hunt County, Texas.

More About Rebecca Tennessee Kimbell:
Burial: Brigham Cemetery, Campbell, Hunt County, Texas
Living In: 1880 Living with her son, Henry, and his children in Precinct 4, Hunt County, Texas

Notes for Rebecca Tennessee Kimbell:
Arrived in Republic of Texas October 1837.

More About Wiley Blunt Brigham:
Burial: Brigham Cemetery, Campbell, Hunt County,
Texas
Living In: 1840 Red River County, Texas
Occupation: 1850 in Precinct 2, Cass County, Texas; Farmer
Occupation: 1860 in Precinct 2, Hunt County, Texas; Farmer
Military Service: 24 May 1841 in Battle of Village Creek; Member of Captain James Bourland's Republic of Texas Militia
Military Service: Bet. 17-29 Sep 1841; Member of Captain Matthew's Lamar County Minutemen
Property: 01 Aug 1837 in Washington, Arkansas; Purchased 40 acres of public land being offered for sale at Washington, Arkansas by the U.S. Government.
Property: 1850 in Cass County, Texas; 90 Acres Improved and 590 Acres Unimproved
Property: 1860 in Hunt County, Texas; 150 Acres Improved and 1500 Acres Unimproved

Notes for Wiley Blunt Brigham:
Arrived in Republic of Texas October 1837.
Name is spelled "Willie Blount Brigham" on August 1, 1837 U.S. Government land sale record.

Wiley Blunt Brigham and Rebecca Tennessee Kimbell had the following children:

52.   i. HENRY[6] BRIGHAM was born in Oct 1839 in Texas. He died in 1919. He married (1) AMELIA J. HALE, daughter of William Reese Hale on 06 Aug 1868. She was born in 1852. She died in 1870. He married (2) ELIZABETH ANN RAWSON, daughter of Charles Rawson and Eliza (unknown) on 07 Apr 1872. She was born on 27 Oct 1848. She died on 26 Feb 1878. He married (3) ELLA T. PITTS on 07 Nov 1886. She was born in 1855. She died in 1912.

     ii.   MARY ANN ELIZABETH BRIGHAM was born about 1843 in Texas. She married Frank J. Beard on 03 Jan 1861.

     iii.   REBECCA TENNESSEE BRIGHAM was born about 1845 in Texas. She married James R. Baker on 04 Jul 1861.

     iv.   ROBERT P. BRIGHAM was born on 24 Nov 1847 in Texas. He died on 01 Dec 1860 in Hunt County, Texas.

More About Robert P. Brigham:
Burial: Brigham Cemetery, Campbell, Hunt County, Texas

29.   **ALBERT GALLATIN**[5] **KIMBELL** (Joseph[4], Benjamin[3], Benjamin[2], William[1]) was born on 20 Jan 1817 in (near) Nashville, Tennessee. He died on 20 Jun 1899 in Perris, California. He married Sarah Castain Gleaves on 12 Oct 1841 in Red River County, Republic of Texas. She was born on 15 May 1825 in Davidson county, Tennessee. She died on 02 Dec 1880 in California.

More About Albert Gallatin Kimbell:
Living In: 1867 San Joaquin, California
Living In: 29 Sep 1868 Sacramento, California
Living In: 1879 Los Angeles, California
Living In: 1890 San Francisco, California
Living In: 1892 Los Angeles, California
Living In: 1896 Los Angeles, California
Occupation: 14 Nov 1850 in Marin County, California; Farmer
Occupation: Bet. 1860-1861; Assistant Marshall in San Francisco, California
Occupation: 1860 in San Francisco, California; Clerk
Occupation: 1870 in Oakland, California; R. E. Clerk
Occupation: 187 ; Farmer, Los Angeles County, California

Notes for Albert Gallatin Kimbell:
Probably arrived in Republic of Texas in September 1838.
Joined the California Gold Rush of 1849, arriving by ship at San Francisco in January 1850. Went to Cochise County, Arizona from 1880 to 1883 as a miner.

More About Sarah Castain Gleaves:
Burial: Evergreen Cemetery, Los Angeles, California
Living In: 1880 Living with her son, William, and her other children in El Monte, Los Angeles County, California.

Albert Gallatin Kimbell and Sarah Castain Gleaves had the following children:

53.   i. JOHN FELIX[6] KIMBELL was born on 23 Jan 1843 in Lamar County, Republic of Texas. He died on 20 May 1893 in California. He married Margaret Elizabeth Turner, daughter of John Gilead Rupe Turner and Hester Ann Megee in 1874. She was born on 07 Jan 1852 in Fannin County, Texas. She died on 21 Nov 1895 in Pottawatomie County, Oklahoma.

     ii. MARY E . KIMBELL was born on 31 Dec 1844 in Austin, Republic of Texas. She married William C. Harrington in 1864 in San Francisco, California.

     iii. WILLIAM YOUNG KIMBELL was born on 10 Jan 1847 in Austin, Texas.

More About William Young Kimbell:
Occupation: 1879; Farmer, Los Angeles County, California
Occupation: 1880 in El Monte, Los Angeles County, California; Farmer

iv.   ALBERT THOMAS KIMBELL was born on 23 Oct 1849 in Austin, Texas.

More About Albert Thomas Kimbell:
Living In: 1880 Living with his brotrher, William, in El Monte, Los Angeles County, California.
Occupation: 1879 in Los Angeles County, California; Farmer
Occupation: 1880 in El Monte, Los Angeles County, California;
Farmer
Occupation: 1885 in Perris Valley, California; Farmer
Occupation: 1886 in Los Angeles, California; Storekeeper
Occupation: 1890 in Perris Valley, California; Farmer
Occupation: 04 Nov 1898 in 4th District, Riverside County, California;
County Supervisor

v.   FRANK G. KIMBELL was born on 06 Jun 1854 in California. He died on 07 Jan 1859.

vi.   HENRY S. KIMBELL was born in May 1856 in California. He died on 11 Sep 1857.

vii.   CHARLES J. KIMBELL was born on 09 Jul 1858 in San Francisco, California.

viii.   EDWARD G. KIMBELL was born on 20 Dec 1860 in California.

More About Edward G. Kimbell:
Occupation: 1880 in El Monte, Los Angeles County, California; Farmer

ix.   EUGENE L. KIMBELL was born on 01 Jan 1863 in California. He died on 13 May 1950 in Riverside, California. He married IDA M. (UNKNOWN). She was born in 1869. She died in 1943.

More About Eugene L. Kimbell:
Burial: Olivewood Cemetery, Riverside, Riverside County, California

x.   SALLIE R. KIMBELL was born on 17 Jan 1865 in San Francisco, California. She married C. H. COWLES.

xi.   SAMUEL B. KIMBELL was born on 02 Mar 1867 in San Francisco, California.

30.   **WILLIAM H.**[5] **KIMBELL** (Joseph[4], Benjamin[3], Benjamin[2], William[1]) was born in 1822 in Tennessee. He died on 01 May 1853 in Austin, Texas. He married Rebecca A. (unknown) about 1848. She was born on 17 Sep 1833 in Tennessee. She died on 19 Dec 1908 in Texas.

More About William H. Kimbell:
Living In: 1850 William, Rebecca and Temperance are living with the wife of his brother, Albert, and her children in Austin, Texas.
Occupation: 1850 in Austin, Travis County, Texas; Clerk

More About Rebecca A. (unknown):
Burial: High Grove Cemetery, Bastrop County, Texas

Living In: 1855 Bastrop County, Texas
Living In: 1856 Bastrop County, Texas

William H. Kimbell and Rebecca A. (unknown) had the following children:

    i.   TEMPERANCE E.[6] KIMBELL was born about 1849.

    ii.   MOLLIE KIMBELL was born about 1851.

    iii.   SARAH HOLIDAY KIMBELL was born about 1853.

31.   JOSEPH E.[5] STURDIVANT (Rebecca[4] Kimbell, Benjamin[3] Kimbell, Benjamin[2] Kimbell, William[1] Kimbell) was born in 1808 in Warren County, North Carolina. He died in 1876 in Marion County, Texas. He married **NANCY ANN COOPWOOD**. She was born about 1815.

More About Nancy Ann Coopwood:
Living In: 1880 Cass County, Texas with her son Marshall K. Sturdivant.

Joseph E. Sturdivant and Nancy Ann Coopwood had the following children:

    i.   MARSHALL K.[6] STURDIVANT was born in Jan 1839 in Mississippi.

    More About Marshall K. Sturdivant:
    Living In: 1860 Marion County, Texas
    Living In: 1870 Davis County, Texas (Cass County, Texas after 1873)
    Living In: 1880 Cass County, Texas
    Living In: 1900 Cass County, Texas
    Occupation: Physician

    ii.   ANNE E. STURDIVANT was born about 1845 in Mississippi.

    More About Anne E. Sturdivant:
    Occupation: 1870; School Teacher

    iii.   MARY E. STURDIVANT was born about 1846 in Mississippi.

    iv.   ELLA STURDIVANT was born about 1850 in Mississippi.

    v.   WILLIAM C. STURDIVANT was born about 1852 in Mississippi.

    vi.   ALICE STURDIVANT was born in Jan 1857 in Mississippi.

    More About Alice Sturdivant:
    Living In: 1900 As a widow in Cass County, Texas, with her brother Marshall K. Sturdivant.

32.   MARTHA FRANCES[5] KIMBELL (John Mosely[4], Benjamin[3], Benjamin[2], William[1]) was born about 1826 in Halifax County, North Carolina. She died in 1896 in Mississippi. She married **REDDING HERVEY**.

Redding Hervey and Martha Frances Kimbell had the following children:

    i.   JOHN[6] HERVEY.

    ii.   LAURA HERVEY.

54.   iii. SAMUEL BROWN HERVEY was born in 1852. He married Alice Parks McLarty in Mississippi.

          iv.   JOSEPH HERVEY.

          v.   MARGARET HERVEY.

33.   **SALLY ANN^5 KIMBELL** (John Mosely^4, Benjamin^3, Benjamin^2, William^1) was born about 1832 in Halifax County, North Carolina. She died in 1852 in Mississippi. She married Lafayette L. Moore about 1848 in Halifax County, North Carolina.

Lafayette L. Moore and Sally Ann Kimbell had the following child:
     i.   DAVID^6 MOORE was born about 1850. He died before 1880.

34.   **WILLIAM^5 KIMBELL** (Benjamin^4, David^3, Benjamin^2, William^1) was born in 1805 in North Carolina. He married **MARY HENTON**.

William Kimbell and Mary Henton had the following child:
     i.   WHITMAN HILL^6 KIMBELL.

35.   **JOHN THOMAS^5 KIMBELL** (Gideon^4, David^3, Benjamin^2, William^1) was born on 12 Jan 1814 in Oglethorpe County, Georgia. He died on 05 Jul 1899. He married Mary Pittman Lumpkin on 27 Mar 1834 in Georgia. She was born on 16 Mar 1810. She died on 26 Jan 1888 in Georgia.

More About John Thomas Kimbell:
Occupation: ; Baptist Minister

John Thomas Kimbell and Mary Pittman Lumpkin had the following children:
     i.   WILLIAM JOSEPH^6 KIMBELL was born on 17 May 1835. He married ANTINET A. CURRY.

     ii. JAMES GIDEON KIMBELL was born on 01 May 1837. He married Frances Sims on 24 Nov 1857.

     iii. JOHN PITTMAN KIMBELL was born on 29 Mar 1840. He died on 02 May 1862.

     iv. HENRY BEASLEY KIMBELL was born on 05 Mar 1842. He died in Aug 1891.

     v. FRANCIS TIMOTHY KIMBELL was born on 26 Mar 1844. He married Mary Tingle on 17 Dec 1867.

36.   **MARY C.^{5} KIMBELL** (Edmond^4, James^3, Benjamin^2, William^1) was born about 1805. She married Peyton H. Lyles in 1824.

Peyton H. Lyles and Mary C. Kimbell had the following child:
     i.   SAMUEL^6 LYLES was born about 1830.

         More About Samuel Lyles:
         Burial: Kimbell Cemetery, Decatur, Alabama

37.   **FRANCES A.^{5} KIMBELL** (Edmond^4, James^3, Benjamin^2, William^1) was born on 31 Jan 1817. She died on 15 Aug 1859. She married **JOHN PATRICK MOSELEY**.

More About Frances A. Kimbell:
Burial: Kimbell Cemetery, Decatur, Alabama

John Patrick Moseley and Frances A. Kimbell had the following children:

    i. ANN ELIZABETH[6] MOSELEY was born on 04 Apr 1835. She died on 12 Oct 1869. She married Lucian Minor on 22 Jul 1853.

        More About Ann Elizabeth Moseley:
        Burial: Kimbell Cemetery, Decatur, Alabama

    ii. EDMOND KIMBELL MOSELEY was born about May 1845. He died on 06 Sep 1849.

        More About Edmond Kimbell Moseley: Burial:
        Kimbell Cemetery, Decatur, Alabama

    iii. MARY OPHELIA MOSELEY was born about Mar 1840. She died on 04 Sep 1845.

        More About Mary Ophelia Moseley:
        Burial: Kimbell Cemetery, Decatur, Alabama

38. MARY P.[5] KIMBELL (Nathan[4], James[3], Benjamin[2], William[1]) was born in 1814. She married EDWARD LOGWOOD. She married ATABALPA COLUMBUS STUART.

Edward Logwood and Mary P. Kimbell had the following child:

    i. MARY ELIZABETH[6] LOGWOOD. She married ATABALPA COLUMBUS STUART.

39. REBECCA M.[5] MORRISS (Elizabeth Lee[4] Armistead, Rebecca[3] Kimbell, Benjamin[2] Kimbell, William[1] Kimbell) was born in Randolph County, North Carolina. She died on 08 Sep 1862 in Clarke County, Alabama. She married THOMAS BOROUGHS. He was born on 11 Aug 1803 in North Carolina. He died on 02 Nov 1866 in Clarke County, Alabama.

Thomas Boroughs and Rebecca M. Morriss had the following children:

    i. MARTHA JANE BOROUGHS was born on 15 Jan 1838 in Clarke County, Alabama. She died on 17 Jun 1903 in Clarke County, Alabama. She married THOMAS ISHAM KIMBELL. He was born on 10 May 1829 in Clarke County, Alabama. He died on 11 Feb 1914 in Clarke County, Alabama.

    ii. ANN ELIZABETH BOROUGHS was born on 16 Sep 1830 in Clarke County, Alabama. She died on 07 Jun 1908. She married HENLEY WASHINGTON COATES. He was born in Clarke County, Alabama. She married JAMES ADDISON NEWMAN. He was born in Orange County, Virginia.

    iii. THOMAS J. BOROUGHS was born on 18 Apr 1832 in Clarke County, Alabama. He died on 01 Jun 1893. He married MARY CAROLINE SMITH. She was born in Clarke County, Alabama.

    iv. WILLIAM MORRIS BOROUGHS was born on 22 Feb 1835 in Clarke County, Alabama.

He died on 15 Aug 1909. He married LAURA JENKINS. She was born in Monroe County, Alabama.

v.   MARY LOUISE BOROUGHS was born on 07 Dec 1843 in Clarke County, Alabama. She died on 25 Feb 1891.

vi.   BRYAN BOROUGHS was born on 14 May 1847 in Clarke County, Alabama. He married Mary Elizabeth Dickinson, daughter of James Shelton Dickinson in Oct 1871.

   More About Bryan Boroughs:
   Occupation: Physician

vii.   REBECCA S. BOROUGHS. She married FRANK STALLWORTH. He was born in Conecuh County, Alabama.

Generation 6

40.   **EDWARD BASCOM[6] KIMBELL** (Benjamin Davis[5], Joseph[4], Benjamin[3], Benjamin[2], William[1]) was born on 26 Aug 1848 in Cass County, Texas. He died on 06 Jan 1925 in Whiteflat, Texas. He married Missouri Alice Turner, daughter of John Gilead Rupe Turner and Hester Ann Megee on 12 May 1874 in Milford, Texas. She was born on 13 Nov 1853 in Ellis County, Texas. She died on 17 Apr 1935.

More About Edward Bascom Kimbell:
Occupation: Farmer

Notes for Edward Bascom Kimbell:
Married, along with his brother George Washington Kimbell, in a double wedding ceremony

Edward Bascom Kimbell and Missouri Alice Turner had the following children:

i.   WALTER EDWARD[7] KIMBELL was born on 25 Feb 1875. He died on 11 Oct 1966. He married Florence Western Partin on 27 Apr 1902. She was born on 09 Nov 1883. She died on 12 Sep 1963.

ii.   JOSEPH GILLARD KIMBELL was born on 02 Jul 1876 in Blum, Texas. He died in 1947. He married Lelah Anderson on 09 Apr 1902. She was born on 20 Jul 1881 in Wheeler County, Texas.

iii.   ANNA KIMBELL was born on 11 Jan 1878. She died on 04 Apr 1964 in Whiteflat, Texas. She married GEORGE BAIN. He was born in 1874. He died on 11 Nov 1958 in Lubbock, Texas. She married HENRY HUGHES.

iv.   DELLA KIMBELL was born on 17 Mar 1880 in Georgetown, Texas. She died on 15 Apr 1953. She married (1) SHELLY OTHO ROBBINS in 1901. She married (2) CHARLES EARL HARRIS on 07 May 1927. He died in Aug 1952.

v.   MARY ALICE KIMBELL was born on 24 Nov 1883 in Seymore, Texas. She died on 20 Mar 1974 in Whiteflat, Texas. She married Irvine Donnahue Merrill on 24 Sep 1908 in Whiteflat, Texas.

vi.   TURNER DAVIS KIMBELL was born on 16 Nov 1887 in Texas. He died on 08 Sep

1966 in Odessa, Texas. He married Junie Melvelle Garrison on 06 Jan 1909 in Childress, Texas. She was born on 27 Feb 1888 in Harris County, Texas. She died on 02 Nov 1976.

More About Turner Davis Kimbell:
Burial: 11 Sep 1966 in Matador Cemetery, Matador, Texas
Cause Of Death: Head Injury from Automobile Accident
Occupation: Rancher

vii. LEONA KIMBELL was born on 16 Jun 1890 in Motley County, Texas. She died on 28 Jul 1941 in Austin, Texas.

More About Leona Kimbell:
Burial: Roaring Springs, Texas
Cause Of Death: Upper Respiratory Infection

Notes for Leona Kimbell:
Never Married.

viii. WILLIAM GUY KIMBELL was born on 26 Jul 1895 in Motley County, Texas. He died on 04 Sep 1978. He married Edith Nola Robinson on 30 Oct 1921 in Matador, Texas. She was born on 18 Jan 1898.

More About William Guy Kimbell:
Occupation: Jeweler
Occupation: Watchmaker

41. GEORGE WASHINGTON[6] KIMBELL (Benjamin Davis[5], Joseph[4], Benjamin[3], Benjamin[2], William[1]) was born on 17 Aug 1850 in Cass County, Texas. He died on 10 Jul 1921 in Flomot, Texas. He married (1) CLEMMIE MAXWELL on 12 May 1874 in Milford, Texas. She died in 1884. He married (2) DIXIE RANSONE in 1886. She was born on 09 Nov 1862 in Cleburne, Texas. She died on 23 Sep 1903 in Motley County, Texas.

More About George Washington Kimbell:
Occupation: Farmer

Notes for George Washington Kimbell:
Married, along with his brother Edward Bascom Kimbell, in a double wedding ceremony.

George Washington Kimbell and Clemmie Maxwell had the following children:
i. BENJAMIN LANG[7] KIMBELL was born in 1877. He died on 05 May 1948. He married JENNIE MCLAUGHLIN.

ii. EULA ELIZABETH KIMBELL was born on 04 Dec 1879. She died on 28 Jan 1963. She married S. W. SULLIVAN.

iii. STERLING HENRY KIMBELL was born on 24 Feb 1880 in Johnson County, Texas. He died on 20 Jan 1957 in Quitaque, Texas. He married Leola Boyles on 07 Jan 1911. She died on 06 Sep 1960 in Grange Hall, Texas.

More About Sterling Henry Kimbell:
Occupation: Farmer
Occupation: Well Driller

    iv.   BERTA KIMBELL was born on 26 Feb 1883. She died on 12 Jun 1910. She married SAM WHITE.

George Washington Kimbell and Dixie Ransone had the following children:

    v.   MATTIE MAY KIMBELL was born on 28 Jun 1887. She died in Jun 1912. She married BEN SLOSS.

    vi.   RUBY LEE KIMBELL was born on 28 Jun 1887. She died on 18 Dec 1928. She married WALTER ROBERSON. He was born on 17 Sep 1905. He died on 03 Sep 1966.

    vii.   WILLIE LOU KIMBELL was born on 19 Jan 1890. She died on 15 Jun 1971. She married T. Everitt Boyles on 07 Dec 1913. He died in 1963.

    viii.   ALA GEORGE ANNA KIMBELL was born on 24 Oct 1891. She died on 08 Feb 1959. She married Roscoe Fort on 02 Oct 1910.

    ix.   ROSE EDNA KIMBELL was born on 24 Oct 1891. She died on 24 Jul 1960. She married Floyd Tiffin on 28 Dec 1914.

    x.   BRYAN RANSONE KIMBELL was born on 10 Apr 1896 in Blum, Texas. He died on 29 Jun 1967 in Wilcox, Arizona. He married Catherine Louise Findley on 21 Sep 1919. She was born on 14 Aug 1896 in Canadian, Oklahoma.

    xi.   ROBERT JULIAN KIMBELL was born on 27 Mar 1901. He died on 23 Mar 1903.

    xii.   LOUIS KIMBELL was born on 27 Mar 1901. He died on 30 Mar 1901.

42.   **MATILDA**[6] **KIMBELL** (Benjamin Davis[5], Joseph[4], Benjamin[3], Benjamin[2], William[1]) was born on 29 May 1852. She died on 08 Sep 1888 in Lampasas, Texas. She married **BAILEY BAKER**.

More About Matilda Kimbell:
Burial: Dodson Cemetery, Hill County, Texas

Bailey Baker and Matilda Kimbell had the following child:

    i.   OSCAR HENRY[7] BAKER was born in 1874. He died in 1950 in Muleshoe, Texas. He married JOSIE CHILTON. He married LILLIE (UNKNOWN).

43.   **WILLIAM BAYLESS**[6] **KIMBELL** (Benjamin Davis[5], Joseph[4], Benjamin[3], Benjamin[2], William[1]) was born on 23 May 1865 in Blum, Texas. He died on 12 Jun 1928 in Dimmitt, Texas. He married Margaret Elizabeth Vashti Bankston, daughter of Jackson Washington Bankston and Nancy Elizabeth Thurman on 29 Jan 1891 in Floydada, Texas. She was born on 05 Feb 1869 in Walker County, Georgia. She died on 18 Jul 1936 in Dimmiitt, Texas.

More About William Bayless Kimbell:
Cause Of Death: Heart Attack
Occupation: Abt. 1886; Ranch hand on Matador Ranch.

William Bayless Kimbell and Margaret Elizabeth Vashti Bankston had the following children:

    i. JAMES MORRIS[7] KIMBELL was born on 08 May 1892 in Matador, Texas. He died on 16 May 1961 in Carthage, Missouri. He married Clara V. Jarrett on 16 Sep 1920. She was born on 04 Mar 1903 in Goldwaite, Texas. She died on 17 Jan 1989.

More About James Morris Kimbell:
Cause Of Death: Heart Attack
Occupation: Farmer
Occupation: Worked for Shell Pipeline Company
Military Service: World War One (France)

Notes for James Morris Kimbell:
Played the Violin.

55.   ii. WILLIAM BOYD KIMBELL was born on 23 Dec 1893 in Rio Vista, Texas. He died on 05 Feb 1972 in Portales, New Mexico. He married Mabel Cora Hyatt, daughter of James Elisha Hyatt and Cora Annie Martin on 12 Jun 1917 in Clovis, New Mexico. She was born on 07 Jun 1900 in Beverly, Texas. She died on 13 Apr 1999 in Clovis, New Mexico.

    iii. EDWARD EARL KIMBELL was born on 04 Dec 1895. He died on 15 Dec 1915 in Abilene, Texas.

    iv. LUCILLE BERKLEY KIMBELL was born on 19 Jul 1898 in Matador, Texas. She died on 23 Aug 1964. She married Jesse Adam Savage on 24 Jul 1915. He was born on 14 Nov 1893. He died on 07 Feb 1983.

    v. ANNIE LOIS KIMBELL was born on 26 Aug 1900. She died on 25 Nov 1902.

    vi. JEFFIE KIMBELL was born on 08 Feb 1903. He died on 11 Feb 1903.

    vii. EUGENE THURMAN KIMBELL was born on 18 Feb 1904 in Matador, Texas. He died on 13 Sep 1985 in Plainview, Texas. He married Mary Merrill on 20 Sep 1939. She was born on 27 Sep 1914.

More About Eugene Thurman Kimbell:
Burial: Dimmitt, Texas
Occupation: Farmer
Occupation: Television and Radio Repair

    viii. LEOLA MARGARET KIMBELL was born on 11 Feb 1906. She died on 19 May 1994 in San Antonio, Texas. She married Leonard E. Lankford, son of (unknown) Lankford and Winnie Davis on 01 Sep 1930. He was born on 30 May 1906 in Enid, Oklahoma. He died on 07 Mar 1976 in San Antonio, Texas.

    ix. MAUDE KIMBELL was born on 05 Jun 1908. She died on 06 Jun 1908.

    x. CLAUDE KIMBELL was born on 05 Jun 1908. He died on 17 Jun 1908.

    xi. FANNIE BERNICE KIMBELL was born on 24 May 1909 in Gasoline, Texas. She died on 05 Feb 1973 in Dimmitt, Texas. She married George Blanton on 14 Jul 1935. He was born on 14 May 1901. He died on 10 Feb 1991.

More About Fannie Bernice Kimbell:
Cause Of Death: Heart Trouble

xii.   MABEL EUNICE KIMBELL was born on 24 May 1909 in Gasoline, Texas. She died on
17 Aug 1994 in Amarillo, Texas. She married Virgil Bills on 23 Aug 1936. He
was born on 07 Jun 1907. He died on 28 Jul 1964 in Amarillo, Texas.

xiii.   EDWIN BASCOM KIMBELL was born on 25 Sep 1913 in Gasoline, Texas. He died on
7 Apr 1996 in Dimmitt, Texas. He married Georgia Lee Kaiser on 20 Nov 1948.
She was born on 17 Apr 1918. She died on 27 Sep 1993 in Dimmitt, Texas.

44.   **HELENA TEXANA**[6] **KIMBELL** (Thomas Moody[5], Joseph[4], Benjamin[3], Benjamin[2], William[1]) was
born on 16 Feb 1845 in Hickory Hill, Cass County, Republic of Texas. She died in 1908. She
married Robert Sayle on 28 Sep 1866. He was born on 14 Jan 1831. He died in Jul 1914 in
Greenville, Texas.

More About Helena Texana Kimbell:
Burial: East Mount Cemetery, Greenville, Texas

More About Robert Sayle:
Burial: East Mount Cemetery, Greenville,
Texas
Occupation: Medical Doctor

More About Robert Sayle and Helena Texana
Kimbell: Marriage Fact: Married by John Pattillo

Robert Sayle and Helena Texana Kimbell had the following children:

56.   i.   ANNA ELIZABETH[7] SAYLE was born in Aug 1867. She married JOSEPH BECTON.

57.   ii.   EULALIA SAYLE. She married LOUIS NAPOLEON BYRD.

45.   **MARY ANN ELIZABETH**[6] **KIMBELL** (Thomas Moody[5], Joseph[4], Benjamin[3], Benjamin[2], William[1]) was
born on 23 Dec 1848 in Cass County, Texas. She died on 05 Jul 1881 in Hunt County, Texas.
She married Benjamin Franklin Kelly on 02 Mar 1869 in Hunt County, Texas. He was born on 17
Dec 1844 in Charleston, Virginia. He died on 10 Mar 1896 in Commerce, Texas.

More About Mary Ann Elizabeth Kimbell:
Burial: Lebanon Cemetery, Commerce, Texas

More About Benjamin Franklin Kelly:
Burial: Lebanon Cemetery, Commerce,
Texas
Occupation: School Teacher

Benjamin Franklin Kelly and Mary Ann Elizabeth Kimbell had the following children:

i.   ELIZABETH[7] KELLY was born on 23 Jan 1870. She died on 22 Dec 1871.

58.   ii. WILLIAM MARION KELLY was born on 29 Dec 1872 in Hunt County, Texas. He died on 07
Feb 1951 in Dallas, Texas. He married Mary Lou Harper on 27 Aug 1893 in Texas.
She was born on 15 Mar 1877. She died on 02 Mar 1949 in Dallas, Texas.

    iii.   MINNIE KELLY was born on 19 Sep 1874. She died on 13 Mar 1971. She married GEORGE B. HALL. He was born on 16 Feb 1861. He died on 27 Nov 1924.

    iv.   CHARLIE KELLY was born on 04 Mar 1875. He died on 06 Sep 1875.

    v.   HARRY KELLY was born on 04 Mar 1875. He died on 08 Aug 1876.

    vi.   DAISY MOLLIE KELLY was born on 12 Sep 1877. She died on 15 Feb 1946 in Dallas, Texas. She married Edgar Berry Clifton on 09 Dec 1894 in West Commerce, Texas. He was born on 08 Apr 1870 in Collinsville, Alabama. He died on 09 Apr 1915 in Detroit, Texas.

    vii.   ARTHUR KELLY was born on 12 Dec 1879 in Commerce, Texas. He died on 24 Jul 1968 in Dallas, Texas.

    viii.   ERA KELLY was born on 03 Jun 1881. She died on 06 Sep 1881.

46.   **CHARLES HENRY[6] KIMBELL** (Thomas Moody[5], Joseph[4], Benjamin[3], Benjamin[2], William[1]) was born on 16 Jan 1855 in Cass County, Texas. He died on 20 Oct 1926 in Campbell, Texas. He married Laura Lou Taylor on 16 Aug 1909 in Greenville, Texas. She was born on 25 Aug 1884 in Dukedom, Kentucky. She died on 26 Oct 1982 in Greenville, Texas.

More About Charles Henry Kimbell:
Cause Of Death: Heart Attack

More About Laura Lou Taylor:
Burial: Brigham   Cemetery,   Campbell,
Texas Cause Of Death: Stroke

Charles Henry Kimbell and Laura Lou Taylor had the following children:

    i.   CHARLES HENRY[7] KIMBELL was born on 18 May 1910. He died on 31 Mar 1995 in Campbell, Texas. He married Charlene Adele Roberts on 28 Mar 1942. She was born on 24 Sep 1918.

    More About Charles Henry Kimbell:
    Cause Of Death: Heart Attack
    Occupation: Worked for Greenville, Texas Street Department

    ii.   WILDA ELIZABETH KIMBELL was born on 04 Apr 1913. She married HOWARD T. GREEN. She married HARMON ABBOTT.

    iii.   HATTIE JEAN KIMBELL was born on 28 Sep 1917. She died on 01 Aug 1999 in Campbell, Texas. She married JOHN R. TURNER. She married MIGUEL POMPA.

47.   **MARTHA REBECCA[6] KIMBELL** (Thomas Moody[5], Joseph[4], Benjamin[3], Benjamin[2], William[1]) was born on 30 Sep 1856 in Cass County, Texas. She died on 18 Jul 1888. She married Robert Wright Ridley on 12 Feb 1880. He was born in 1839. He died in 1918.

More About Martha Rebecca Kimbell: Burial:
Brigham Cemetery, Campbell, Texas

More About Robert Wright Ridley:

Burial: Brigham Cemetery, Campbell, Texas

Robert Wright Ridley and Martha Rebecca Kimbell had the following children:

    i.   THOMAS ROBERT[7] RIDLEY was born on 26 Feb 1881 in Campbell, Texas. He died on 22 Oct 1918.

        More About Thomas Robert Ridley:
        Military Service: World War One

        Notes for Thomas Robert Ridley:
        Killed in Action during World War One.

    ii.   LILLIAN RIDLEY was born on 22 Oct 1883. She died on 22 Oct 1883.

    iii.   RUBY LEE RIDLEY was born in 1884. She died in 1974. She married BOYD R. BAGWELL.

59.   iv.   FRED REGINALD RIDLEY was born in 1885. He died in 1971. He married CHLOE HENDERSON.

48.   **ELIZABETH JANE[6] KIMBELL** (John M.[5], Joseph[4], Benjamin[3], Benjamin[2], William[1]) was born on 23 Jul 1843 in DeKalb, Republic of Texas. She died on 08 Feb 1920 in Texarkana, Bowie County, Texas. She married Rhesa Walker Read, son of Martin I. Read and Eliza Walker on 16 Nov 1859 in DeKalb, Texas. He was born on 20 Dec 1836 in Canton, Alabama. He died on 02 Aug 1909 in Texarkana, Bowie County, Texas.

More About Elizabeth Jane Kimbell:
Burial: 10 Feb 1920 in Rose Hill Cemetery, Texarkana, Bowie County, Texas
Living In: 1860 Bowie County, Texas
Living In: 1910 Living with her son in law, Spencer Collom, and his family in Texarkana Ward 1, Bowie County, Texas.

More About Rhesa Walker Read:
Burial: Rose Hill Cemetery, Texarkana, Bowie County, Texas
Occupation: 1860 in Beat 3, Bowie County, Texas; M.D.
Occupation: 02 Jun 1863; Date of Rank as Surgeon with the 29th Texas Cavalry.
Occupation: 1870 in Precinct 4, Bowie County, Texas; Physician
Occupation: 1880 in Bowie County, Texas; Physician
Military Service: Bet. 19 Jul 1862-Apr 1865; 29th Texas Cavalry, C.S.A.

Notes for Rhesa Walker Read:
Graduate of Tulane University (known as Louisiana College at that time) in 1856.
Graduated from Medical Department of University of Pennsylvania in 1858.
Confirmed as Surgeon with the 29th Texas Cavalry, C.S.A. on February 2, 1864, accepted confirmation on July 5, 1864 with date of rank being June 2, 1863.

Rhesa Walker Read and Elizabeth Jane Kimbell had the following children:

60.   i. SARA ETHEL[7] READ was born on 30 Nov 1862 in DeKalb, Texas. She died on 17 Sep 1934 in Bryan, Texas. She married Walter Wipprecht, son of Rudolf Wipprecht and Julia Kapp on 15 Jun 1893 in Brazos County, Texas. He was born on 03 Jan 1864 in Sisterdale, Texas. He died on 28 Sep 1951 in Bryan, Texas.

61.   ii. ADA CAROLINE READ was born on 10 Aug 1867 in DeKalb, Texas. She died on 25 Jun 1955 in Austin, Texas. She married Robert Lee Penn, son of Robert Penn and Sarah Elizabeth Allen on 11 Sep 1889 in Texarkana, Texas. He was born on 13 Sep 1864 in San Felipe, Texas. He died on 03 Sep 1909 in Austin, Texas.

62.   iii. ALBERT CHISHOLM READ was born in Dec 1869 in DeKalb, Texas. He died on 18 Jan 1926 in Little Rock, Arkansas. He married Julia Zimmerman, daughter of Jesse F. Zimmerman and Mary F. (unknown) on 17 Oct 1895 in Bowie County, Texas. She was born in Dec 1871 in Arkansas.

    iv. WILLIAM KIMBELL READ was born on 11 Mar 1871 in New Boston, Texas. He died on 25 Mar 1930 in Texarkana, Texas. He married Julia Williams, daughter of James M. Williams and Larissa Allen in 1895. She was born on 29 Mar 1873 in Camden, Arkansas. She died on 31 Jan 1966 in Dallas, Texas.

More About William Kimbell Read:
Burial: 27 Mar 1930 in Rose Hill Cemetery, Texarkana, Texas
Cause Of Death: Angina Pectoris
Occupation: Medical Doctor

Notes for William Kimbell Read:
Military headstone has "Texas - Major - Medical Corps" on three lines.

63.   v. EUGENIA ELIZABETH READ was born on 15 Feb 1874 in New Boston, Texas. She died on 29 Jun 1969 in Austin, Texas. She married Spencer Allen Collom, son of S. R. Collom on 23 Dec 1896. He was born on 30 Sep 1866 in Bowie County, Texas. He died on 26 Apr 1934 in Texarkana, Texas.

64.   vi. MARY WALKER READ was born on 02 Sep 1876 in Bowie County, Texas. She died on 31 Aug 1941 in Huntsville, Texas. She married Leonard Holmes Bush in 1897. He was born on 23 Dec 1865 in Walker County, Texas. He died on 14 May 1941 in Huntsville, Texas.

    vii. EUNICE READ was born on 13 Oct 1879 in Texas. She died on 15 Oct 1881 in Texas.

More About Eunice Read:
Burial: Read Hill Cemetery, Bowie County, Texas

49.   JULIA REBECCA[6] KIMBELL (John M.[5], Joseph[4], Benjamin[3], Benjamin[2], William[1]) was born on 31 Mar 1845 in Republic of Texas. She died on 26 Jan 1908 in Texas. She married (1) EDWARD WARREN GARLAND, son of Edward Garland and Nancy W. Smiser before 1878. He was born on 28 Oct 1825 in Giles County, Tennessee. He died on 12 May 1897 in Texas. She married (2) WILLIAM J. WYSE, son of James William Wyse and Patience Caroline Baker Teel after 07 May 1865. He was born in 1830 in Louisiana.

More About Julia Rebecca Kimbell:
Burial: Garland Cemetery, Red River County, Texas
Cause Of Death: Infection from a rat bite to her hand while reaching into a corn bin in her barn
Living In: 1900 With her Garland children in Commisioner Precinct 3, Bowie County, Texas
Occupation: 1860 in DeKalb, Texas; Seamstress
Property: 1886 in Bowie County, Texas; 18 Acres

More About Edward Warren Garland:
Burial: Garland Cemetery, Red River County, Texas
Living In: 1845 With his uncle, Peter Garland, in Tishomingo County, Mississippi, two doors
away from the home of Mary Emeline Jenkins
Living In: Feb 1868 Red River County, Texas
Occupation: 1850 in Tishomingo County, Mississippi; Merchant
Occupation: 1880 in Precinct 7, Red River County, Texas; Farmer
Military Service: Bet. 13 Sep 1847-10 Jul 1848 in Mexican War; Company C, Second
Mississippi Infantry, U.S. Army
Military Service: Civil War for C.S.A.
Property: 1869 in Bowie County, Texas; 300 Acres
Property: 1870 in Bowie County, Texas; 300 Acres
Property: 1880 in Red River County, Texas; 36 Acres Improved and 50 Acres
Unimproved
Property: 1888 in Bowie County, Texas; 108 Acres and 8 city lots in DeKalb
Property: 1889 in Bowie County, Texas; 108 Acres and 8 city lots in DeKalb
Property: 1896 in Bowie County, Texas; 110 Acres and 7 city lots in DeKalb
Property: 1897 in Bowie County, Texas; 110 Acres and 7 city lots in DeKalb

Notes for Edward Warren Garland:
Mustered in for Mexican War in Farmington, Mississippi. Mustered out in Vicksburg, Mississippi.

November 25, 1869 Red River County, Texas voter registration shows Edward having lived in
Red River County and Texas 22 months at that time.

Edward Warren Garland and Julia Rebecca Kimbell had the following children:

65.   i. JOSEPH EDWARD[7] GARLAND was born on 17 Mar 1878 in Red River County, Texas. He
died on 01 Sep 1946 in Lamesa, Dawson County, Texas. He married Lou Ethel
Bynum, daughter of Alfred Baker Bynum and Dorinda Sandal Baird on 21 May 1908 in
Brownfield, Texas. She was born on 25 Apr 1890 in Whitewright, Grayson County,
Texas. She died on 17 Sep 1969 in Lamesa, Dawson County, Texas.

66.   ii. EMMA GEORGIE IRENE GARLAND was born on 23 Mar 1880 in Annona, Texas. She died
on 17 Dec 1969 in Kerrville, Texas. She married LeRoy Ardis Edwards in May 1921
in Roscoe, Texas. He was born on 27 Feb 1881 in Sulphur Springs, Texas. He died
on 05 Dec 1951 in Loraine, Texas.

     iii. RUFUS SMIZER MCKINNEY GARLAND was born on 03 Sep 1882 in Texas. He died on 07
Feb 1919 in North Atlantic Ocean (Returning from France after World War One).

More About Rufus Smizer McKinney Garland:
Burial: Loraine, Texas
Cause Of Death: Spanish Flu
Occupation: 1910 in Roscoe, Texas; Drug Store Prescriptionist
Occupation: 1917 in Loraine, Texas; Pharmacist
Military Service: 1918 in France; World War One (Medic)
Military Service: Spanish American War

Notes for Rufus Smizer McKinney Garland:
Died at sea on the way home from World War One military service in France due
to the Great Flu Epidemic.
Never Married.

67.   iv. MAGGIE AUGUSTA ESTELLE GARLAND was born in Aug 1884 in DeKalb, Texas. She died on 29 Jan 1955 in Sweetwater, Texas. She married Barna Haney, son of William Daniel Haney and Mamie H. Harkins on 24 May 1911 in Roscoe, Texas. He was born on 30 Nov 1887 in Temple, Bell County, Texas. He died on 27 Jan 1957 in Roscoe, Texas.

More About William J. Wyse:
Living In: Bet. 1850-1870 DeKalb, Texas
Living In: 17 Jul 1860 Next door to John M. Kimbell and his family in Beat 3, Bowie County, Texas
Occupation: 1860 in Beat 3, Bowie County, Texas; Merchant
Occupation: Bet. 19 Aug 1864-05 Nov 1866 in Dekalb, Texas; Postmaster
Occupation: 1870 in DeKalb, Bowie County, Texas; Merchant
Military Service: Bet. 20 Jul 1862-01 Feb 1864; Company I, 29th Texas Cavalry, C.S.A.

Notes for William J. Wyse:
Enlisted at Clarkesville, DeKalb County, Texas in Company I, 29th Texas Cavalry July 19, 1862 . Mustered in at Clarkesville on July 20, 1862. Discharged due to Chronic Articular Rheumatism on February 1, 1864 at Camp Garland in Choctaw Nation, Indian Territory (present day Oklahoma).

William J. Wyse and Julia Rebecca Kimbell had the following children:

68.   i. ELIZABETH LEE[7] WYSE was born on 03 Jul 1867 in Texas. She died on 08 Nov 1926 in Texas. She married (1) WILLIAM D. COOPER on 05 May 1895 in Bowie County, Texas. He was born in Alabama. She married (2) WILLIAM WESLEY LAWSON, son of Isaiah Hampton Lawson and Mary Jane Hooser on 08 Jan 1911 in New Boston, Texas. He was born on 17 Apr 1854 in Red River County, Texas. He died on 16 Dec 1926 in Annona, Texas.

     ii. WILLIAM JAMES WYSE was born about 1869 in Texas. He died before 01 Jun 1900.

     Notes for William James Wyse:
Murdered at an early age while trying to collect a debt owed his general store.

50.   **MARY EMMA[6] KIMBELL** (John M.[5], Joseph[4], Benjamin[3], Benjamin[2], William[1]) was born on 26 Mar 1847 in Texas. She died on 14 Apr 1922 in Deport, Lamar County, Texas. She married Robert J. Bevill before 15 Jul 1870. He was born on 13 Mar 1847 in Henderson, Tennessee. He died on 09 Jan 1913 in Lamar County, Texas.

More About Mary Emma Kimbell:
Burial: 15 Apr 1922 in Mount Olive Cemetery, Lamar County, Texas
Cause Of Death: Injuries From a Fall
Living In: 1920 Living with her son, Rufus, and his family in Deport, Lamar County, Texas

Notes for Mary Emma Kimbell:
Birth date is from headstone.

More About Robert J. Bevill:
Burial: Mount Olive Cemetery, Lamar County, Texas
Living In: 1870 Robert and Mary are living with Robert's parents in Boston, Bowie County, Texas
Occupation: 1870 in Boston, Bowie County, Texas; Farm Labor

Occupation: 1880 in Precinct 1, Lamar County, Texas; Farmer
Occupation: 1900 in Justice Precinct 1, Lamar County, Texas; Farmer
Occupation: 1910 in Justice Precinct 1, Lamar County, Texas; Farmer

Robert J. Bevill and Mary Emma Kimbell had the following children:

    i.   EMMA[7] BEVILL was born about 1874 in Texas.

69.   ii. ELLA BEVILL was born on 09 Mar 1876 in Texas. She died on 04 Jun 1969 in Paris, Texas. She married Moses Franklin Secrest, son of Issac Secrest and Elizabeth Pyron about 1897. He was born on 19 Jul 1873 in Monroe, North Carolina. He died on 22 Sep 1947 in Paris, Texas.

    iii.   ROBERT EMMETT BEVILL was born on 20 May 1878 in Lamar County,Texas. He died on 15 Aug 1964 in Contra Costa County, California. He married Aletha Della DeWese on 15 Oct 1898 in Paris, Texas. She was born on 15 Feb 1880 in Lamar County, Texas. She died on 08 Mar 1974 in Brentwood, California.

    More About Robert Emmett Bevill:
    Burial: Brentwood Cemetery, Brentwood, Contra Costa County, California

    iv.   JAMES ALBERT BEVILL was born on 30 Apr 1883 in Texas. He died on 11 Sep 1970 in Paris, Texas. He married KATIE BECKHAM. She was born on 29 Aug 1881 in Texas. She died on 04 Jul 1968 in Paris, Texas.

    More About James Albert Bevill:
    Burial: 14 Sep 1970 in Evergreen Cemetery, Paris, Lamar County, Texas
    Cause Of Death: Cerebral Hemorrhage
    Living In: 1910 Living with his parents in Justice Precinct 1, Lamar County, Texas.
    Occupation: 1910 in Justice Precinct 1, Lamar County, Texas; Farmer
    Occupation: Produce and Cafe Operator

    v.   RUFUS BEVILL was born on 27 Apr 1886 in Texas. He died on 01 Oct 1977 in Texas. He married ANNA HORN. She was born on 09 Dec 1888 in Marion County, Alabama. She died on 02 Feb 1970 in Paris, texas.

    More About Rufus Bevill:
    Burial: Evergreen Cemetery, Paris, Lamar County, Texas
    Living In: 1910 Living with his parents in Justice Precinct 1, Lamar County, Texas.
    Occupation: 1910 in Justice Precinct 1, Lamar County, Texas; Farmer
    Occupation: 1920 in Deport, Lamar County, Texas; Grocery Store Merchant

51.   **EMILY MATILDA[6] KIMBELL** (John M.[5], Joseph[4], Benjamin[3], Benjamin[2], William[1]) was born in 1850 in DeKalb, Bowie County, Texas. She died on 13 Apr 1928 in Texarkana, Bowie County, Texas. She married James Joseph Peters, son of Lemuel Peters and Elizabeth (unknown) on 16 Apr 1874 in Bowie County, Texas. He was born on 17 Dec 1843 in Bowie County, Texas. He died on 10 Apr 1925 in New Boston, Texas.

More About Emily Matilda Kimbell:
Burial: 13 Apr 1928 in Read Hill Cemetery, New Boston, Bowie County, Texas
Cause Of Death: Fracture of Femur (from death certificate)

Occupation: 1870 in Precinct 4, Bowie County, Texas; School Teacher

More About James Joseph Peters:
Burial: 12 Apr 1925 in Read Hill Cemetery, New Boston, Bowie County,
Texas
Living In: Bet. 1843-1925 Bowie County, Texas
Living In: 1870 Living with his mother in Boston, Bowie County, Texas
Occupation: 1870 in Boston, Bowie County, Texas; Farm Laborer
Occupation: 1880 in Bowie County, Texas; Justice of the Peace
Occupation: 1900 in Commissioner Precinct 2, Bowie County, Texas; Justice of the
Peace
Occupation: 1910 in Justice Precinct 2, Bowie County, Texas; Justice of the Peace
Occupation: 1920 in New Boston, Bowie County, Texas; Justice of the Peace
Military Service: Bet. 25 Jan 1862-27 Mar 1864; Company E, 32nd Texas Dismounted
Cavalry, C.S.A.
Military Service: Bet. 27 Mar 1864-07 Jun 1865; Company G, 3rd Texas Cavalry, C.S.A.

Notes for James Joseph Peters:
   Enlisted January 25, 1862 in Company E. 32nd Texas Dismounted Cavalry, C.S.A. and
transferred to Company G, 3rd Texas Cavalry C.S.A. after a wound received at Elkhorn Tavern,
Arkansas (May 7-8, 1862) made him unable to serve on foot. After being wounded James was
put on medical leave and sent home until March 1864.
   Company G, 3rd Texas Cavalry was surrendered on May 26, 1865 at New Orleans, Louisiana by
General E. K. Smith, C.S.A. James Peters was paroled June 7, 1865 at Shreveport, Louisiana.

James Joseph Peters and Emily Matilda Kimbell had the following children:

  i. LEMUEL KIMBELL [7] PETERS was born on 25 Apr 1875 in New Boston, Texas. He died on
    04 Apr 1951 in Kilgore, Gregg County, Texas. He married EFFIE HELEN OWENS. She
    was born on 22 Jul 1878 in Lamar County, Texas. She died on 07 Jul 1967 in Kilgore,
    Gregg County, Texas.

    More About Lemuel Kimbell Peters:
    Burial: 05 Apr 1951 in Kilgore City Cemetery, Kilgore, Gregg County,
    Texas Cause Of Death: Heart Failure
    Occupation: Hardware Salesman

  ii. WALTON E. PETERS was born in Jan 1878 in Texas. He died on 06 Nov 1906.

    More About Walton E. Peters:
    Burial: Read Hill Cemetery, New Boston, Bowie County, Texas

70. iii. PAUL MITCHELL PETERS was born on 28 Feb 1882 in Nerw Boston, Texas. He died on 10
    Apr 1954 in Longview, Texas. He married SARAH EMMALYN FOSHEE. She was born on
    18 Nov 1881 in Texas. She died on 08 Jul 1946 in Gregg County, Texas.

  iv. EBBYE PETERS was born on 12 Oct 1883 in New Boston, Bowie County, Texas. She
    died on 03 Jun 1972 in New Boston, Bowie County, Texas. She married (UNKNOWN)
    OLIVER.

    More About Ebbye Peters:
    Burial: 05 Jun 1972 in Read Hill Cemetery, New Boston, Bowie County, Texas
    Living In: 1910 Living with her parents in Justice Precinct 2, Bowie County, Texas
    Occupation: 1910 in Justice Precinct 2, Bowie County, Texas; Sales Lady in
    General Store

    v.   WILLIE ADA PETERS was born on 04 Oct 1884 in New Boston, Bowie County, Texas. She died on 18 Aug 1968 in Texarkana, Bowie County, Texas. She married VIVIAN HOLMES JAMES. He was born on 24 Sep 1880 in Wolfe City, Hunt County, Texas. He died on 10 Jun 1954 in Texarkana, Bowie County, Texas.

    More About Willie Ada Peters:
Burial: 20 Aug 1968 in Read Hill Cemetery, New Boston, Bowie County, Texas

    vi.   MAUDE PETERS was born in 1888 in Texas. She died in 1956. She married William R. Roberts, son of J. D. Roberts and Mary Etta Mcglasson on 20 Apr 1910 in Bowie County, Texas. He was born on 24 May 1879 in Jackson County, Tennessee. He died on 05 Aug 1957 in New Boston, Bowie County, Texas.

    More About Maude Peters:
Burial: Read Hill Cemetery, New Boston, Bowie County, Texas

52.   HENRY[6] BRIGHAM (Rebecca Tennessee[5] Kimbell, Joseph[4] Kimbell, Benjamin[3] Kimbell, Benjamin[2] Kimbell, William[1] Kimbell) was born in Oct 1839 in Texas. He died in 1919. He married (1) AMELIA J. HALE, daughter of William Reese Hale on 06 Aug 1868. She was born in 1852. She died in 1870. He married (2) ELIZABETH ANN RAWSON, daughter of Charles Rawson and Eliza (unknown) on 07 Apr 1872. She was born on 27 Oct 1848. She died on 26 Feb 1878. He married (3) ELLA T. PITTS on 07 Nov 1886. She was born in 1855. She died in 1912.

More About Henry Brigham:
Burial: Brigham Cemetery, Campbell, Hunt County, Texas
Occupation: 1880 in Precinct 4, Hunt County, Texas; Farmer

More About Amelia J. Hale:
Burial: Brigham Cemetery, Campbell, Hunt County, Texas
Cause Of Death: Tuberculosis

Henry Brigham and Amelia J. Hale had the following child:

71.   i.   AMELIA VIRGINIA[7] BRIGHAM was born on 03 Feb 1870. She married ROBERT BARNETT.

More About Elizabeth Ann Rawson:
Burial: Brigham Cemetery, Campbell, Hunt County, Texas

Henry Brigham and Elizabeth Ann Rawson had the following children:

    ii.   WILLIAM H. BRIGHAM was born about 1873 in Texas.

    iii.   GEORGE R. BRIGHAM was born about 1875 in Texas.

    iv.   ELISA R. BRIGHAM was born about 1878 in Texas.

More About Ella T. Pitts:
Burial: East Mount Cemetery, Greenville, Hunt County, Texas

More About Henry Brigham and Ella T. Pitts:
Marriage Fact: Divorced

53.   JOHN FELIX[6] KIMBELL (Albert Gallatin[5], Joseph[4], Benjamin[3], Benjamin[2], William[1]) was born on 23 Jan 1843 in Lamar County, Republic of Texas. He died on 20 May 1893 in California. He married Margaret Elizabeth Turner, daughter of John Gilead Rupe Turner and Hester Ann Megee in 1874. She was born on 07 Jan 1852 in Fannin County, Texas. She died on 21 Nov 1895 in Pottawatomie County, Oklahoma.

More About John Felix Kimbell:
Occupation: 1860 in San Francisco, California; Apprentice to Machinist

More About Margaret Elizabeth Turner:
Burial: Walker Cemetery, Pottawatomie County, Oklahoma

John Felix Kimbell and Margaret Elizabeth Turner had the following children:

   i.   ALBERT JOHN[7] KIMBELL was born on 23 May 1875.

73.   ii. JOSEPHUS CHARLES KIMBELL was born on 19 Jul 1876. He died on 20 Jan 1948. He married Annie Elizabeth White on 17 Nov 1901. She was born on 11 Jul 1884 in Pattawatomie County, Oklahoma. She died on 08 Jul 1953.

      iii. GEORGE TURNER KIMBELL was born on 28 Jan 1878. He died on 23 Sep 1961. He married Bertie Helm about 1909.

73.   iv. MARY MARGARET KIMBELL was born on 31 Jul 1879. She died on 31 Jan 1936. She married David P. Bains about 1900. He was born in Mar 1868 in Tennessee.

      v.   PEARL ALICE KIMBELL was born on 22 Dec 1881. She died on 11 Nov 1951. She married Jacob Edward Mangold on 03 Oct 1907 in Oklahoma. He was born on 25 Jul 1881 in Kerrville, Texas. He died on 13 Sep 1922 in Oklahoma.

      vi. LAURA ANNIE KIMBELL was born on 22 May 1883. She died on 22 Dec 1977.

      vii. CHRIS WEBB KIMBELL was born on 07 Nov 1884. He died on 22 May 1979. He married Beulah (unknown) about 1908. She was born about 1880 in Oklahoma.

      viii. LILLIAN GLEAVES KIMBELL was born on 26 Aug 1887. She died on 13 Nov 1918.

      ix. SAM PAUL JONES KIMBELL was born on 11 Jun 1889. He died on 31 Jul 1911.

54.   SAMUEL BROWN[6] HERVEY (Martha Frances[5] Kimbell, John Mosely[4] Kimbell, Benjamin[3] Kimbell, Benjamin[2] Kimbell, William[1] Kimbell) was born in 1852. He married Alice Parks McLarty in Mississippi.

Samuel Brown Hervey and Alice Parks McLarty had the following children:

   i.   IDA[7] HERVEY.

      ii. ANNIE HERVEY.

      iii. CHARLIE HERVEY.

75.   iv. RUTH HERVEY. She married JOHN S. THROOP.

Generation 7

55. **WILLIAM BOYD**[7] **KIMBELL** (William Bayless[6], Benjamin Davis[5], Joseph[4], Benjamin[3], Benjamin[2], William[1]) was born on 23 Dec 1893 in Rio Vista, Texas. He died on 05 Feb 1972 in Portales, New Mexico. He married Mabel Cora Hyatt, daughter of James Elisha Hyatt and Cora Annie Martin on 12 Jun 1917 in Clovis, New Mexico. She was born on 07 Jun 1900 in Beverly, Texas. She died on 13 Apr 1999 in Clovis, New Mexico.

More About William Boyd Kimbell:
Occupation: Farmer
Occupation: Carpenter

William Boyd Kimbell and Mabel Cora Hyatt had the following children:

   i.   BERNICE LUCILLE[8] KIMBELL was born on 23 Nov 1918 in Hart, Texas. She married Wallace William Fields on 04 Jul 1939. He was born in 1921. He died in 1970.

   ii. ROSALIE INEZ KIMBELL was born on 21 Sep 1920 in Dimmitt, Texas. She died on 10 May 2001 in Alamogordo, New Mexico. She married Charles Norwell Anderson on 20 Jul 1940 in Portales, New Mexico. He was born on 02 Dec 1919 in Cone, Texas.

        More About Rosalie Inez Kimbell:
        Cause Of Death: Complications (infection) from hip surgery.

   iii. OWEN BOYD KIMBELL was born on 24 Jan 1922 in Dimmitt, Texas. He died on 18 Mar 1998 in Lubbock, Texas. He married Wilma Jean Anderson on 31 Aug 1945. She was born on 13 Dec 1926 in Portales, New Mexico.

        More About Owen Boyd Kimbell:
        Burial: 20 Mar 1998 in Portales, New Mexico
        Cause Of Death: Cancer
        Occupation: Owned and operated City Motor Company in Lovington, New Mexico.
        Military Service: U. S. Army, World War Two

        Notes for Owen Boyd Kimbell:
        Served in Europe with the U.S. Army during World War Two.

   iv. EARL WESLEY KIMBELL was born on 23 May 1923. He died on 24 May 1923.

   v.   WOODY W. KIMBELL was born on 14 Mar 1924. He died on 14 Mar 1924.

   vi. RAYWORTH ELLIS KIMBELL was born on 09 Jul 1925 in Dimmitt, Texas. He died on 02 May 2001 in Hobbs, New Mexico. He married Wanda Colleen Bennett on 20 Jun 1960. She was born on 28 Nov 1931.

        More About Rayworth Ellis Kimbell:
        Burial: 05 May 2001 in Lovington Cemetery, Hobbs, New Mexico
        Cause Of Death: Cancer
        Military Service: Bet. 1943-1946; U.S. Navy

        Notes for Rayworth Ellis Kimbell:
        Served on U.S.S. Enterprise (CV46) 1943-1945.

    vii.   RUTH MARILYN KIMBELL was born on 13 Jan 1930 in Dimmitt, Texas. She married Carol Morgan Charles, son of Joe Charles and Lois Jackson on 03 Jun 1951 in Portales, New Mexico. He was born on 11 Jan 1931 in Loraine, Texas.

       More About Ruth Marilyn Kimbell:
       Occupation: Elementary School Teacher

    viii. IVIS WELDON KIMBELL was born on 21 Nov 1931 in Dimmitt, Texas. She died on 05 Nov 1956 in Texas.

       More About Ivis Weldon Kimbell:
       Cause Of Death: Automobile Accident
       Military Service: Bet. 1951-1953; U. S. Army, Korean War

       Notes for Ivis Weldon Kimbell:
       Graduated from O.C.S. as a Second Lieutenant.

    ix.   REX ELTON KIMBELL was born on 09 Jun 1936 in Portales, New Mexico. He married Bette Alice McDermaid on 06 Aug 1968. She was born on 25 Jul 1946 in Portales, New Mexico.

       More About Rex Elton Kimbell:
       Military Service: Bet. 1954-1957 ; U.S. Navy

56.   **ANNA ELIZABETH**^{7} **SAYLE** (Helena Texana^6 Kimbell, Thomas Moody^5 Kimbell, Joseph^4 Kimbell, Benjamin^3 Kimbell, Benjamin^2 Kimbell, William^1 Kimbell) was born in Aug 1867. She married **JOSEPH BECTON**.

More About Joseph Becton:
Occupation: Medical Doctor

Joseph Becton and Anna Elizabeth Sayle had the following children:

    i.   JOSEPH^8 BECTON.

       More About Joseph Becton:
       Occupation: Medical Doctor

    ii.   MAMIE BECTON.

    iii.   ANNA BECTON.

57.   **EULALIA**^{7} **SAYLE** (Helena Texana^6 Kimbell, Thomas Moody^5 Kimbell, Joseph^4 Kimbell, Benjamin^3 Kimbell, Benjamin^2 Kimbell, William^1 Kimbell, Robert). She married **LOUIS NAPOLEON BYRD**.
Louis Napoleon Byrd and Eulalia Sayle had the following children:

    i.   LUCILLE^8 BYRD.

    ii.   LOUISE BYRD.

    iii.   ROBERT BYRD.

58.   **WILLIAM MARION**[7] **KELLY** (Mary Ann Elizabeth[6] Kimbell, Thomas Moody[5] Kimbell, Joseph[4] Kimbell, Benjamin[3] Kimbell, Benjamin[2] Kimbell, William[1] Kimbell) was born on 29 Dec 1872 in Hunt County, Texas. He died on 07 Feb 1951 in Dallas, Texas. He married Mary Lou Harper on 27 Aug 1893 in Texas. She was born on 15 Mar 1877. She died on 02 Mar 1949 in Dallas, Texas.

More About William Marion Kelly:
Burial: Forest Park Cemetery, Greenville, Texas

More About Mary Lou Harper:
Burial: Forest Park Cemetery, Greenville, Texas

William Marion Kelly and Mary Lou Harper had the following children:

     i.   ROBERT MARION[8] KELLY was born on 05 Nov 1894 in Commerce, Texas. He died on 18 Dec 1985 in Denton, Texas. He married GERTRUDE ONEAL VAN HUSS. She was born on 12 May 1900 in Durant, Oklahoma. She died on 05 Apr 1972 in Dallas, Texas. He married (2) MYRTLE HASHER about 1985.

     ii.   MAMIE LOU KELLY was born on 24 Oct 1896 in Hunt County, Texas. She died on 29 Mar 1920 in Merit, Texas.

     iii.   SAMMY REBECCA KELLY was born on 13 Apr 1899 in Scatter Branch, Texas. She died on 30 Apr 1971 in Dallas, Texas. She married William Francis Griffits on 26 Feb 1944.

     iv.   CHARLES HENRY KELLY was born on 31 Dec 1900 in Campbell, Texas. He died on 15 Jul 1978 in Dallas, Texas. He married Frankie Louise Grey on 10 Jun 1925 in Fort Worth, Texas. She was born on 07 Oct 1904 in Kansas City, missouri. She died on 23 Dec 1992 in Dallas, Texas.

     v.   WILLIAM MARION KELLY was born on 12 May 1908 in Nevada, Texas. He died on 18 Aug 1966 in Dallas, Texas. He married Bertha Frankie Holt on 10 Nov 1928 in Royce City, Texas.

     vi.   GEORGE B. KELLY was born on 28 Sep 1910 in Nevada, Texas. He died on 12 Feb 1977 in Dallas, Texas. He married (1) MARGARET GIERTRUDE HAMMER on 25 Mar 1930 in Durant, Oklahoma. She was born on 09 Feb 1911. She died on 29 Dec 1957 in Dallas, Texas. He married (2) CHARLOTTE NEAL on 08 Mar 1959 in Dallas, Texas. She was born on 27 Mar 1934.

59.   **FRED REGINALD**[7] **RIDLEY** (Martha Rebecca[6] Kimbell, Thomas Moody[5] Kimbell, Joseph[4] Kimbell, Benjamin[3] Kimbell, Benjamin[2] Kimbell, William[1] Kimbell) was born in 1885. He died in 1971. He married **CHLOE HENDERSON**.

Fred Reginald Ridley and Chloe Henderson had the following children:

     i.   ROBERT HENDERSON[8] RIDLEY was born on 27 Jan 1911 in Campbell, Texas. He died on 06 Jan 1996 in Greenville, Texas. He married MARGARET LOW.

     ii.   DORIS RIDLEY was born about 1913.

     iii.   MARY DELL RIDLEY was born about 1915.

     iv.   ELIZABETH RIDLEY was born about 1917.

v.   CAROLINE RIDLEY was born about 1919.

60.   SARA ETHEL[7] READ (Elizabeth Jane[6] Kimbell, John M.[5] Kimbell, Joseph[4] Kimbell, Benjamin[3] Kimbell, Benjamin[2] Kimbell, William[1] Kimbell) was born on 30 Nov 1862 in DeKalb, Texas. She died on 17 Sep 1934 in Bryan, Texas. She married Walter Wipprecht, son of Rudolf Wipprecht and Julia Kapp on 15 Jun 1893 in Brazos County, Texas. He was born on 03 Jan 1864 in Sisterdale, Texas. He died on 28 Sep 1951 in Bryan, Texas.

More About Sara Ethel Read:
Burial: 18 Sep 1934 in Bryan City Cemetery, Bryan, Brazos County, Texas

Notes for Sara Ethel Read:
Headstone and death certificate give her first name as Sallie.

More About Walter Wipprecht:
Burial: 29 Sep 1951 in Bryan City Cemetery, Bryan, Brazos County, Texas
Cause Of Death: Coronary Thrombosis
Occupation: Fiscal Department of Texas ANC

Walter Wipprecht and Sara Ethel Read had the following children:

    i.   IDA[8] WIPPRECHT.

    ii.   READ WIPPRECHT.

    iii.   CARL WIPPRECHT.

    iv.   WALTER WIPPRECHT.

61.   ADA CAROLINE[7] READ (Elizabeth Jane[6] Kimbell, John M.[5] Kimbell, Joseph[4] Kimbell, Benjamin[3] Kimbell, Benjamin[2] Kimbell, William[1] Kimbell) was born on 10 Aug 1867 in DeKalb, Texas. She died on 25 Jun 1955 in Austin, Texas. She married Robert Lee Penn, son of Robert Penn and Sarah Elizabeth Allen on 11 Sep 1889 in Texarkana, Texas. He was born on 13 Sep 1864 in San Felipe, Texas. He died on 03 Sep 1909 in Austin, Texas.

More About Ada Caroline Read:
Burial: 27 Jun 1955 in Oakwood Cemetery, Austin, Texas

More About Robert Lee Penn:
Burial: Oakwood Cemetery, Austin, Texas
Occupation: Abt. 1889; City Attorney of Taylor, Texas
Occupation: Sep 1899; Judge in Williamson County, Texas
Occupation: Mar 1900; Judge of the 53rd District, State of Texas

Robert Lee Penn and Ada Caroline Read had the following children:

    i.   ROBERT READ[8] PENN was born on 23 Jul 1890 in Taylor, Texas. He died on 19 Dec 1931 in Bledsoe, Texas. He married Elizabeth Hudson on 03 Jun 1916 in Belton, Texas. She was born on 17 Dec 1889 in Belton, Texas. She died in Dec 1981 in Dallas, Texas.

    More About Robert Read Penn:
    Burial: 21 Dec 1931 in Grove Hill Memorial Park, Dallas, Texas
    Cause Of Death: Accidental Gunshot Wound

Occupation: President of Penn Oil Company

ii.   DONALD MITCHELL PENN was born on 16 Aug 1892 in Taylor, Texas. He died on 27
      Mar 1973 in Midland, Texas. He married (1) BELLE WORKS, daughter of W. W.
      Works and Belle McWhorter on 25 Dec 1917. She was born on 14 Mar 1895 in
      Texas. She died on 21 Jun 1923 in Dallas, Texas. He married (2) CATHERINE ALICE
      SHIPLEY, daughter of William A. Shipley and Elizabeth Sutherland in 1926. She
      was born on 03 Sep 1902 in Dennison, Texas. She died on 09 Dec 1962 in
      Lubbock, Texas.

      More About Donald Mitchell Penn:
      Burial: 28 Mar 1973 in Trinity Memorial Park, Big Spring,
      Texas
      Cause Of Death: Cerebral Thrombosis
      Occupation: Lumberman

iii. RHESA LEE PENN was born on 27 Jul 1894 in Taylor, Texas. He died on 15 Dec
      1960 in Temple, Texas. He married Hildur Linnea Peterson on 10 Oct 1920 in
      San Marcos, Texas. She was born on 27 Jun 1900 in Austin, Texas. She died on
      12 Jul 1994 in Austin, Texas.

      More About Rhesa Lee Penn:
      Burial: Oakwood Cemetery, Austin, Texas

iv.   EUGENE DOAK PENN was born on 29 Jan 1896 in Taylor, Texas. He died on 20
      May 1918 in (near) Loggia, Italy.

      More About Eugene Doak Penn:
      Burial: Oakwood Cemetery, Austin, Texas

      Notes for Eugene Doak Penn:
      Died in a training accident (near Loggia, Italy) as an Aviation Cadet in the
      Allied Expeditionary Force during World War One.
      Promoted to 1st Lieutenant May 16, 1918.

v.   ALBERT WILLIAM PENN was born on 28 Sep 1897 in Taylor, Texas. He died on
      09 Nov 1985 in Austin, Texas. He married Myrle Myrle Shelley on 27 Nov 1930
      in Austin, Texas. She was born on 29 Aug 1906. She died on 30 Dec 2001.

      More About Albert William Penn:
      Burial: Oakwood Cemetery, Austin, Texas

vi.   ELIZABETH PENN was born on 17 May 1900 in Austin, Texas. She died on 17 Jul
      1978 in Austin, Texas. She married Thomas Edward Johnson on 06 Nov 1927
      in Austin, Texas. He was born on 25 Mar 1899 in Texas. He died on 22 Oct
      1987 in Austin, Texas.

vii. MARIAN PENN was born on 14 Sep 1904 in Austin, Texas. She died on 04 Aug
      1989 in Austin, Texas. She married Marion West Fowler on 05 Mar 1926 in
      Austin, Texas. He was born on 28 Sep 1901 in Farmersville, Texas. He died on
      13 Nov 1994 in Austin, Texas.

     viii.   SARAH PENN was born on 26 Oct 1906 in Austin, Texas. She died in 2004. She married John Stuart Harris on 29 Jan 1927 in Austin, Texas. He was born on 30 Sep 1903. He died on 09 May 1976 in Austin, Texas.

     ix.   WILLIAM Y. PENN was born on 21 Sep 1908 in Austin, Texas. He died on 26 Jul 1996 in Midland, Texas. He married Addilee Lancaster on 16 Jan 1939 in Midland, Texas. She was born on 18 Oct 1908 in Midland, Texas. She died in Jun 1985 in Midland, Texas.

62.   **ALBERT CHISHOLM^7 READ** (Elizabeth Jane^6 Kimbell, John M.^{5} Kimbell, Joseph^4 Kimbell, Benjamin^3 Kimbell, Benjamin^2 Kimbell, William^1 Kimbell) was born in Dec 1869 in DeKalb, Texas. He died on 18 Jan 1926 in Little Rock, Arkansas. He married Julia Zimmerman, daughter of Jesse F. Zimmerman and Mary F. (unknown) on 17 Oct 1895 in Bowie County, Texas. She was born in Dec 1871 in Arkansas.

More About Albert Chisholm Read:
Living In: 1900 Albert and Julia are living with her parents in Little Rock, Arkansas
Occupation: 1900 - Druggist

Albert Chisholm Read and Julia Zimmerman had the following children:

     i.   ALBERT CHISOLM^8 READ was born on 14 Mar 1902 in Little Rock, Arkansas. He died in Aug 1974 in Arkansas.

     ii.   VERTNER READ was born in 1906. He married Cora Adel Wallace on 12 Feb 1938.

63.   **EUGENIA ELIZABETH^7 READ** (Elizabeth Jane^6 Kimbell, John M.^{5} Kimbell, Joseph^4 Kimbell, Benjamin^3 Kimbell, Benjamin^2 Kimbell, William^1 Kimbell) was born on 15 Feb 1874 in New Boston, Texas. She died on 29 Jun 1969 in Austin, Texas. She married Spencer Allen Collom, son of S. R. Collom on 23 Dec 1896. He was born on 30 Sep 1866 in Bowie County, Texas. He died on 26 Apr 1934 in Texarkana, Texas.

More About Eugenia Elizabeth Read:
Burial: 30 Jun 1969 in Rose Hill Cemetery, Texarkana,
Texas Cause Of Death: Cerebrovascular Accident

More About Spencer Allen Collom:
Burial: 28 Apr 1934 in Rose Hill Cemetery, Texarkana,
Texas
Cause Of Death: Coronary Occlusion
Living In: 1910 Texarkana Ward 1, Bowie County, Texas
Occupation: Medical Doctor

Spencer Allen Collom and Eugenia Elizabeth Read had the following children:

     i.   MINNIE ELIZABETH^8 COLLOM was born on 21 Oct 1897 in Texarkana, Texas. She married Gamewell D. Gantt on 19 Oct 1921.

     ii.   FRANCES MARTHA COLLOM was born on 16 Feb 1899 in Texarkana, Texas. She married (1) JAMES FREDERICK WARREN on 14 Jun 1922 in Bowie County, Texas. She married WILBER J. HILL.

     iii.   ALLEN READ COLLOM was born in 1901. He died in 1903.

     iv.   SPENCER ALLEN COLLOM was born on 04 Feb 1904 in Ratcliff, Texas.

64.   **MARY WALKER**[7] **READ** (Elizabeth Jane[6] Kimbell, John M.[5] Kimbell, Joseph[4] Kimbell, Benjamin[3] Kimbell, Benjamin[2] Kimbell, William[1] Kimbell) was born on 02 Sep 1876 in Bowie County, Texas. She died on 31 Aug 1941 in Huntsville, Texas. She married Leonard Holmes Bush in 1897. He was born on 23 Dec 1865 in Walker County, Texas. He died on 14 May 1941 in Huntsville, Texas.

More About Mary Walker Read:
Burial: 01 Sep 1941 in Oakwood Cemetery, Huntsville, Texas

More About Leonard Holmes Bush:
Burial: 15 May 1941 in Oakwood Cemetery, Huntsville, Texas
Occupation: Medical Doctor

Leonard Holmes Bush and Mary Walker Read had the following children:

      i.   KATHERINE[8] BUSH.

      ii.   LEONARD EWING BUSH.

      iii.   MARY BUSH.

65.   **JOSEPH EDWARD**[7] **GARLAND** (Julia Rebecca[6] Kimbell, John M.[5] Kimbell, Joseph[4] Kimbell, Benjamin[3] Kimbell, Benjamin[2] Kimbell, William[1] Kimbell) was born on 17 Mar 1878 in Red River County, Texas. He died on 01 Sep 1946 in Lamesa, Dawson County, Texas. He married Lou Ethel Bynum, daughter of Alfred Baker Bynum and Dorinda Sandal Baird on 21 May 1908 in Brownfield, Texas. She was born on 25 Apr 1890 in Whitewright, Grayson County, Texas. She died on 17 Sep 1969 in Lamesa, Dawson County, Texas.

More About Joseph Edward Garland:
Burial: 03 Sep 1946 in Lamesa Cemetery, Lamesa, Texas
Cause Of Death: Cerebral Hemorrhage
Living In: 1900 With his mother and siblings in Bowie County, Texas
Occupation: 1900 in Commissioner Precinct 3, Bowie County, Texas; Day Laborer
Occupation: 1910 in Dawson County, Texas; Lawyer
Occupation: 1918 in Lamesa, Texas; County Judge and Attorney
Occupation: 1920 in Lamesa, Texas; Attorney at Law
Occupation: 1930 in Lamesa, Texas; Independant Lawyer
Occupation: 1940 in Lamesa, Texas; Attorney at Law
Military Service: Spanish American War

More About Lou Ethel Bynum:
Burial: 19 Sep 1969 in Lamesa Cemetery, Lamesa, Texas Cause Of Death: Heart Disease

Joseph Edward Garland and Lou Ethel Bynum had the following children:

      i.   EDWARD BYNUM[8] GARLAND was born on 15 Jun 1909 in Texas. He died on 30 Oct 1986 in Seminole, Texas.

          More About Edward Bynum Garland:
          Burial: Lamesa Cemetery, Lamesa, Texas
          Living In: 1930 Living with his parents in Lamesa, Texas
          Living In: 1940 Living with his parents in Lamesa, Texas

Occupation: 1940 in Lamesa, Dawson County, Texas; Stock Farmer
Military Service: Bet. 05 Sep 1942-15 Nov 1945; U.S. Army, World War Two

ii.   MARGARET DORINDA GARLAND was born on 01 Oct 1911 in Lamesa, Dawson County, Texas. She died on 29 Apr 2005 in Lubbock, Texas. She married James Mack Noble, son of James Mack Noble and Rosia Lee Carter on 01 Jan 1933 in Lamesa, Texas. He was born on 29 Jun 1898 in Texas. He died on 07 Sep 1961 in O'Donnell, Texas.

More About Margaret Dorinda Garland:
Burial: 03 May 2005 in O'Donnell Cemetery, O'Donnell, Texas

Notes for Margaret Dorinda Garland:
      Lubbock Avalanche-Journal
Obituary of Margaret Garland Noble
Published: Monday, May 02, 2005

Margaret Garland Noble, 93, of Lubbock and formerly of ODonnell died Friday, April 29, 2005 at Grace House in Lubbock. She was born Sept. 30, 1911 in Lamesa. She married James Mack Noble, Jr. Jan. 1, 1933 in Lamesa. He preceded her in death in 1961.

Mrs. Noble was the daughter of Joseph Edward and Ethel Garland, who were early pioneer settlers in Dawson and Lynn counties. She was a world traveler, seeing places like China, Australia, New Zealand and Central America. In 1981, she and her family traveled to Scandanavia and Russia.

Margaret was employed by the U.S. Postal Service as a mail carrier. She belonged to Tuesday Bridge and Study Club in ODonnell.

Two brothers, James and Edward, also precede her in death.

Survivors include: two sons, Edward Garland of San Francisco Bay Area, Calif. and James Mack, III of Longview; two grandchildren; and two great-grandchildren.

Services will be 4 p.m. Tuesday at First United Methodist Church in ODonnell with the Rev. Kenneth Peterson officiating.

Burial will be in ODonnell Cemetery.

The family suggests memorial to the ODonnell Cemetery Association or a charity of choice.

Birth date is from birth certificate.
----

iii. JAMES GARLAND was born on 20 Sep 1918 in Lamesa, Dawson County, Texas. He died on 25 Feb 1988 in Hobbs, New Mexico. He married (1) EVA MAE WATERS on 01 Jun 1950 in Dawson County, Texas. She was born about 1924. He married DOROTHY (UNKNOWN).

More About James Garland:
Burial: Dawson County Cemetery, Lamesa, Dawson County, Texas
Occupation: 1940 in Honolulu, Hawaii Territory; Medical Department, Tripler

General Hospital, U.S. Army
Military Service: Bet. 1940-1945; World War Two

Notes for James Garland:
Present during Japanese attack on Pearl Harbor, December 7, 1941.
Served in Europe- Normandy to V.E. Day.
Divorced from Eva Waters on January 16, 1974 in Gaines County, Texas.

66. **EMMA GEORGIE IRENE**[7] **GARLAND** (Julia Rebecca[6] Kimbell, John M.[5] Kimbell, Joseph[4] Kimbell, Benjamin[3] Kimbell, Benjamin[2] Kimbell, William[1] Kimbell) was born on 23 Mar 1880 in Annona, Texas. She died on 17 Dec 1969 in Kerrville, Texas. She married LeRoy Ardis Edwards in May 1921 in Roscoe, Texas. He was born on 27 Feb 1881 in Sulphur Springs, Texas. He died on 05 Dec 1951 in Loraine, Texas.

More About Emma Georgie Irene Garland:
Burial: 20 Dec 1969 in Loraine Cemetery,Loraine, Texas
Cause Of Death: Bronchial Pneumonia and Arteriosclerosis
Living In: 1920 Lamesa, Texas with sister Estelle and family.
Occupation: 1920 in Lamesa, Texas; Teacher

More About LeRoy Ardis Edwards:
Burial: 07 Dec 1951 in Loraine Cemetery, Loraine,
Texas Cause Of Death: Carcinoma of Lung
Occupation: 1930 in Loraine, Texas; Lumber Yard Manager
Occupation: 1940 in Olton, Texas; Retail Lumber Yard Manager

Notes for LeRoy Ardis Edwards:
Discovered and owned, with his brother Walter, "Baking Powder" gold mine in New Mexico.

LeRoy Ardis Edwards and Emma Georgie Irene Garland had the following child:

    i.   ROY GARLAND[8] EDWARDS was born on 30 May 1922 in Loraine, Texas. He died on 14 Oct 1974 in Tampa, Florida. He married Maribel Savage on 08 Apr 1944 in Lubbock, Texas. She was born on 22 Jun 1926 in Sherman, texas. She died on 14 Feb 2010 in Tampa, Florida.

    More About Roy Garland Edwards:
    Burial: Pleasant Grove Cemetery, Durant, Florida
    Cause Of Death: Heart Failure
    Military Service: Bet. 1942-1964; U.S. Air Force (Major)

67. **MAGGIE AUGUSTA ESTELLE**[7] **GARLAND** (Julia Rebecca[6] Kimbell, John M.[5] Kimbell, Joseph[4] Kimbell, Benjamin[3] Kimbell, Benjamin[2] Kimbell, William[1] Kimbell) was born in Aug 1884 in DeKalb, Texas. She died on 29 Jan 1955 in Sweetwater, Texas. She married Barna Haney, son of William Daniel Haney and Mamie H. Harkins on 24 May 1911 in Roscoe, Texas. He was born on 30 Nov 1887 in Temple, Bell County, Texas. He died on 27 Jan 1957 in Roscoe, Texas.

More About Maggie Augusta Estelle Garland:
Burial: 31 Jan 1955 in Roscoe Cemetery, Roscoe,
Texas Cause Of Death: Cerebral Hemorrhage
Living In: 1910 Living with her brother, Rufus Garland, in Roscoe, Texas
Living In: 1920 Lamesa, Texas

Living In: 1930 Roscoe, Texas
Living In: 1955 Roscoe, Texas
Occupation: 1910 in Roscoe, Texas; Dry Goods Saleslady

More About Barna Haney:
Burial: 28 Jan 1957 in Roscoe Cemetery, Roscoe,
Texas
Living In: 1900 Bell County, Texas
Living In: 1910 Living with his parents in Roscoe, Texas
Occupation: 1910 in Roscoe, Texas; Furniture Sales Clerk
Occupation: 1920 in Lamesa, Texas; Clerk in Meyers Drug Company
Occupation: 1930 in Roscoe, Texas; Druggist in Drug Store
Occupation: 1932 in Roscoe, Texas; President of Board of Education
Occupation: 1940 in Roscoe, Texas; Pharmacist and Drug Store owner, Roscoe, Texas

Notes for Barna Haney:
Owned Haney Drug Store, Roscoe, Texas. Mayor and School Board Member of Roscoe, Texas.

More About Barna Haney and Maggie Augusta Estelle Garland:
Marriage License: 23 May 1911 in Nolan County, Texas
Marriage Fact: Married by Rev. J. W. Smith, M. E. Church South, Roscoe, Texas.

Barna Haney and Maggie Augusta Estelle Garland had the following children:

    i. WILLIAM GARLAND[8] HANEY was born on 11 May 1912 in Roscoe, Texas. He died on 19 Jan 1988 in Lubbock, Texas. He married Allie Pearl Dunn, daughter of Yanks Dunn and Ada Branson on 04 Oct 1942 in Roscoe, Texas. She was born on 07 Oct 1922 in Burleson, Texas. She died on 29 Apr 2007 in Roscoe, Texas.

    More About William Garland Haney:
    Burial: Roscoe Cemetery, Roscoe, Texas
    Living In: 1940 Living with his parents in Roscoe, Texas
    Occupation: 1940 in Roscoe, Texas; Retail Drug Clerk
    Occupation: Pharmacist
    Military Service: Enlisted at Lubbock, Texas, January 15, 1942 in U.S. Army for World War Two

    Notes for William Garland Haney:
    Held rank of SSgt. while in U.S. Army.

    ii. MARY JULIA HANEY was born on 16 Aug 1916. She died on 25 Jun 1996 in Clarkesville, Texas. She married Joseph Dellinger Garland, son of Wirt Robert Garland and Lola Prudence Dellinger on 21 Jun 1942 in Roscoe, Texas. He was born on 07 Dec 1914 in Annona, Texas. He died on 16 Aug 1973 in Clarkesville, Texas.

    More About Mary Julia Haney:
    Burial: 29 Jun 1996 in Garland Cemetery, Annona, Texas
    Living In: 1940 Living with her parents in Roscoe, Texas.
    Occupation: 1940 in Roscoe, Texas; Music Teacher
    Occupation: Music Teacher, Pianist, Organist

68.   **ELIZABETH LEE**[7] **WYSE** (Julia Rebecca[6] Kimbell, John M.[5] Kimbell, Joseph[4] Kimbell, Benjamin[3] Kimbell, Benjamin[2] Kimbell, William[1] Kimbell) was born on 03 Jul 1867 in Texas. She died on 08

Nov 1926 in Texas. She married (1) **W**ILLIAM **D. C**OOPER on 05 May 1895 in Bowie County, Texas. He was born in Alabama. She married (2) **W**ILLIAM **W**ESLEY **L**AWSON, son of Isaiah Hampton Lawson and Mary Jane Hooser on 08 Jan 1911 in New Boston, Texas. He was born on 17 Apr 1854 in Red River County, Texas. He died on 16 Dec 1926 in Annona, Texas.

More About Elizabeth Lee Wyse:
Burial: Annona Cemetery, Annona, Red River County, Texas
Occupation: 1900 in Commissioner Precinct 3, Bowie County, Texas; Teacher
Occupation: 1910 in DeKalb, Texas; Public School Teacher

Notes for Elizabeth Lee Wyse:
Living next door to her mother in 1900.
There is a W. D. Cooper in the 1900 U.S. census, born May 1856 in Alabama with an occupation of saloon keeper, living a few houses away from Elizabeth and her son.

William D. Cooper and Elizabeth Lee Wyse had the following child:

i. WYSE DILLARD[8] COOPER was born on 05 Mar 1896 in DeKalb, Texas. He died on 19 May 1926 in Dallas, Texas. He married (1) LUCILE MARTIN, daughter of Thomas Arlander Martin and Curtis Amanda Julia Reagan on 17 Sep 1918 in Mitchell County, Texas. She was born on 08 Jun 1900 in Texas. She died on 25 Oct 1918 in Abilene, Texas. He married (2) MARIE A. BRITTON on 26 Jul 1925 in Johnson County, Texas.

More About Wyse Dillard Cooper:
Burial: 21 May 1926 in Annona Cemetery, Annona,
Texas Cause Of Death: Bronchial Pneumonia
Living In: 1920 Lamesa, Texas in the household of Barna Haney and his family.
Occupation: Jun 1917 in Loraine, Mitchell County, Texas; Tailor
Occupation: 1920 in Lamesa, Texas; Cotton Buyer
Military Service: Bet. 06 Mar 1918-25 Jan 1919; U.S. Army World War One

Notes for Wyse Dillard Cooper:
Enlisted with U.S. Army in Colorado City, Texas March 6,
1918. Promoted to sergeant November 15, 1918.
Service number was 502,124.
Served in Coast Artillery School Det., Fort Monroe, Virginia from May 5, 1918 until January 25, 1919.

More About William Wesley Lawson:
Burial: 17 Dec 1926 in Annona Cemetery, Red River County, Texas
Occupation: 1920 in Justice Precinct 8, Red River County, Texas; Cotton Buyer

More About William Wesley Lawson and Elizabeth Lee Wyse:
Marriage License: 06 Jan 1911 in Bowie County, Texas
Marriage Fact: Marriage Ceremony performed by Reverend Nathan Powell

69. **E**LLA[7] **B**EVILL (Mary Emma[6] Kimbell, John M.[5] Kimbell, Joseph[4] Kimbell, Benjamin[3] Kimbell, Benjamin[2] Kimbell, William[1] Kimbell) was born on 09 Mar 1876 in Texas. She died on 04 Jun 1969 in Paris, Texas. She married Moses Franklin Secrest, son of Issac Secrest and Elizabeth Pyron about 1897. He was born on 19 Jul 1873 in Monroe, North Carolina. He died on 22 Sep 1947 in Paris, Texas.

More About Ella Bevill:
Burial: 07 Jun 1969 in Evergreen Cemetery, Paris, Lamar County, Texas
Cause Of Death: Cardiac Failure

More About Moses Franklin Secrest:
Burial: 24 Sep 1947 in Evergreen Cemetery, Paris, Lamar County, Texas
Cause Of Death: Rupture of Colon
Living In: 1900 Lamar County, Texas
Living In: 1910 Blossom, Lamar County, Texas
Living In: 1930 Smackover, Union County, Arkansas
Living In: 1947 Paris, Lamar County, Texas
Occupation: 1947 - Merchant Grocer
Occupation: 1900 - Farmer
Occupation: 1930 - Foreman at Oil and Water Company
Occupation: 1910 - General Foreman at Truck Farm

Moses Franklin Secrest and Ella Bevill had the following child:

    i.   HELEN PYRON[8] SECREST was born about 1905 in Texas.

70.   PAUL MITCHELL[7] PETERS (Emily Matilda[6] Kimbell, John M.[5] Kimbell, Joseph[4] Kimbell, Benjamin[3] Kimbell, Benjamin[2] Kimbell, William[1] Kimbell) was born on 28 Feb 1882 in Nerw Boston, Texas. He died on 10 Apr 1954 in Longview, Texas. He married SARAH EMMALYN FOSHEE. She was born on 18 Nov 1881 in Texas. She died on 08 Jul 1946 in Gregg County, Texas.

More About Paul Mitchell Peters:
Burial: 12 Apr 1954 in Kilgore City Cemetery, Kilgore, Gregg County, Texas
Cause Of Death: Carcinoma of Lung
Occupation: 1910 in Hugo, Choctaw County, Oklahoma; 1910 - Pipe Line Inspector
Occupation: 1920 in Hugo, Choctaw County, Oklahoma; Commercial Salesman
Occupation: 1930 in Wewoka, Seminole County, Oklahoma; Pipe Fitter with Oil Company
Occupation: (on death certificate) Deputy Tax Assessor Collector

More About Sarah Emmalyn Foshee:
Occupation: 1930 - Circulation manager of Daily Newspaper

Notes for Sarah Emmalyn Foshee:
Known as "Sallie".

Paul Mitchell Peters and Sarah Emmalyn Foshee had the following children:

    i.   LEONARD[8] PETERS was born about 1905 in Texas.

    ii.   ROBERT PETERS was born about 1907 in Texas.

71.   AMELIA VIRGINIA[7] BRIGHAM (Henry[6], Rebecca Tennessee[5] Kimbell, Joseph[4] Kimbell, Benjamin[3] Kimbell, Benjamin[2] Kimbell, William[1] Kimbell) was born on 03 Feb 1870. She married ROBERT BARNETT.

Robert Barnett and Amelia Virginia Brigham had the following child:

    i.   COE J.[8] BARNETT. He married BESS ROBERTSON.

72.   JOSEPHUS CHARLES[7] KIMBELL (John Felix[6], Albert Gallatin[5], Joseph[4], Benjamin[3], Benjamin[2], William[1]) was born on 19 Jul 1876. He died on 20 Jan 1948. He married Annie Elizabeth White on

17 Nov 1901. She was born on 11 Jul 1884 in Pattawatomie County, Oklahoma. She died on 08 Jul 1953.

Josephus Charles Kimbell and Annie Elizabeth White had the following children:

 i. ERNEST NEWTON[8] KIMBELL was born on 19 Sep 1902 in Colorado. He died in 1919.

 ii. CLAUD ALLEN KIMBELL was born on 13 Sep 1904 in Oklahoma. He died in Oct 1979.

 iii. MARGUERITTE ETHEL KIMBELL was born on 26 Aug 1907 in New Mexico.

 iv. JOE LOYD KIMBELL was born on 21 Oct 1909 in New Mexico.

 v. LOTTIE MAE KIMBELL was born on 08 Jul 1913.

 vi. DILLY WINIFRED KIMBELL was born on 17 Jul 1918.

73. **MARY MARGARET[7] KIMBELL** (John Felix[6], Albert Gallatin[5], Joseph[4], Benjamin[3], Benjamin[2], William[1]) was born on 31 Jul 1879. She died on 31 Jan 1936. She married David P. Bains about 1900. He was born in Mar 1868 in Tennessee.

David P. Bains and Mary Margaret Kimbell had the following children:

 i. J.[8] BAINS was born about 1901 in Texas.

 ii. PHILLIP R. BAINS was born about 1904 in Texas.

 iii. BEULAH BAINS was born about 1907 in Texas.

 iv. ARLIE O. BAINS was born about 1910 in New Mexico.

 v. ELVA BAINS was born about 1913.

74. **RUTH[7] HERVEY** (Samuel Brown[6], Martha Frances[5] Kimbell, John Mosely[4] Kimbell, Benjamin[3] Kimbell, Benjamin[2] Kimbell, William[1] Kimbell, Samuel Brown[6], Redding). She married **JOHN S. THROOP**.

John S. Throop and Ruth Hervey had the following child:

 i. JOHN S.[8] THROOP.

www.ingramcontent.com/pod-product-compliance
Lightning Source LLC
Chambersburg PA
CBHW080816280726
48660CB00018B/3473